MW01613417

Common Sense Investing Guide to Retirement

A Comprehensive Guide to Achieving Your Perfect Retirement

Victor James McClure
McClure Capital, Inc.
McClure Capital Advisors, Inc.

Victor James McClure / McClure Capital & McClure Capital Advisors
One Cowboys Way, Suite 570
Frisco, TX 75034
ilovemyretirement.com
commonsenseinvesting.com

Book layout ©2021 Advisors Excel, LLC

Common Sense Investing Guide to Retirement Planning
Victor James McClure, 1st Edition

ISBN 9798432614957

"The investor's chief problem—even his worst enemy—is likely to be himself."
— Benjamin Graham

"An investment in knowledge always pays the best interest."
— Benjamin Franklin

"Formal education will make you a living; self-education will make you a fortune."
— Jim Rohn

"I will tell you how to become rich. Close the doors, be fearful when others are greedy. Be greedy when others are fearful."
— Warren Buffett

Dedicated to my father,
J.R. McClure

Table of Contents

The Importance of Planning

My father, Jimmy Ray McClure, was a successful businessman and one of the greatest salesmen I've ever met. It took me a while to realize it, but he was also one of the greatest influences in my life. He taught me the value of hard work and to never quit. His motto was that any problem could always be solved by working harder and smarter.

His family picked cotton in Greenville, Texas, and was extremely poor. He knew he wanted more, so he started working odd jobs at a very early age to take care of his parents and seven younger siblings. Although he had no formal education beyond the sixth grade, he was very intelligent, hard working, and driven.

When he was fifteen, he could afford a car and started working as a fry cook in Dallas. The roads weren't great back then, so the sixty-mile drive took a long time. But the commute back and forth didn't deter him from showing up day after day and breaking a sweat working over a hot grill.

From there, he started selling different products door to door. The first thing he sold was women's lingerie. Yes, I said it: women's lingerie door to door! Can you imagine that in today's world?

His next door-to-door venture was Great Books, which are similar to encyclopedias. He was so successful at the job that he became the general manager of the entire southwest region of the country at a very young age.

Still wanting more and never being satisfied, he then started selling commodities. Once again, he quickly moved up the ladder. After a short time, he started his own company with fifty brokers under him. He was very successful until his semi-retirement in his fifties.

Through all the twists and turns, a common theme in my father's various career paths is that he always took care and supported everyone: his parents, siblings, and his children. He never complained. He just figured that's just what a good person does. He even bought his mother her first brick house, and when you're poor in Greenville, Texas, owning a brick home is a big deal.

My dad was also a gambler and speculator, so it wasn't a big surprise that he retired in Las Vegas. He chose to invest in commodities, because there was much more upside than stocks. He didn't care about the risk. The excitement and challenge of picking winners really appealed to him.

Having a gambling mentality didn't work out so well for my dad. He went from being a very successful business owner living in a beautiful home in Dallas to living in a dilapidated condo in Vegas alone with his cat. He was very proud and didn't tell me that he had Stage 4 lung cancer until close to the end. As soon as I heard, I flew to Vegas to get him and his belongings and moved him into my house. He ended up dying of cancer a short time later.

Why am I sharing all of this? To show that it doesn't matter how intelligent, honest, and hard working you are, how much you've saved, or how successful you might be. My father had all of those traits in spades. It doesn't matter that you have the greatest intentions and you've spent your life taking care of others. Without proper planning, you can lose everything.

I've devoted my entire life to helping ensure others don't have to go through what my father did. My life's mission is to educate everyone within shouting distance on the importance of proper planning. I want everyone to know that saving for and getting to retirement is a marathon. It's not a sprint. It's long and it's hard.

Once you get close, I often recommend being conservative and securing as much guaranteed income as you can. You can still speculate if you prefer, but don't risk more than you're comfortable losing. Don't let emotions like greed or personal biases get in the way. That's the only way to help ensure you'll maintain your lifestyle throughout your entire existence.

I will continue my mission until I die to help as many people as I can achieve the dream of a financially sound retirement.

The McClure Capital Difference

At the McClure Capital companies, we employ a different kind of retirement strategy. We base everything on math and time-tested planning methods, not our opinion of what the future might hold. Many advisors will tell you what you *want* to hear. They attract clients by promising, "Everything's going to be fine —*if*, of course, you employ our management team."

We take a completely different approach. We tell you what you *need* to hear. As painful as it may be, you need to know the truth, so any shortcoming can be addressed and planned for. I'll give you an example: firms that provide a written retirement plan often use long-term averages of the stock and bond market and apply those averages to the size of your portfolio. Some will use averages of hand-picked indexes or mutual funds. Some will take your expenses and add inflation and taxes to the mix.

Sounds like a pretty good plan, right? The issue is that long-term averages have no bearing on what happen in the future, or what the economic world might look like currently.

As of the writing of the book, the 100-year average of the stock market is around 10 percent. The 100-year average of

10-Year Treasuries is 5 or 6 percent.[1] So, if you took a standard 50/50 portfolio (50 percent stocks, 50 percent bonds), you would have averaged around 8 percent per year over the past 100 years.

Here is the flaw in that type of retirement plan. From 2001 to 2021, the stock market averaged 8.3 percent per year[2] and 10-Year Treasuries around 3.25 percent per year.[3] That same 50/50 portfolio would have only averaged around 5.75 percent during the past 20 years. At the end of 2021, the return on long bonds is even lower—in the 1.45 percent range—so going forward, your returns could be significantly less.[4]

That's before taxes and inflation. It also completely ignores the "sequence of returns risk," which is one of the single biggest risks a retiree will face, in my opinion.

Sequence of Returns Risk

To illustrate sequence of returns risk, imagine you take a $1 million portfolio and need 5 percent per year withdrawn for expenses (or $50,000).

Let's say that the market drops 50 percent once during the first few years of retirement. Your $1 million is now $500,000. You still need to pay your expenses, so it's now down to $450,000. No matter what the market makes going forward, it is virtually impossible to recoup your losses. You're more than likely going to deplete your life savings too quickly. Even if you made 20 percent per year for the next five years in a row, and you still needed $50K per year for expenses, your

[1] CNN Money. "How do bond returns compare with stock returns?" https://money.cnn.com/retirement/guide/investing_bonds.moneymag/index3.htm

[2] Macro Trends. Dec. 27, 2021. "S&P 500 Historical Annual Returns." https://www.macrotrends.net/2526/sp-500-historical-annual-returns

[3] Macro Trends. Dec. 23, 2021. "10 Year Treasury Rate – 54 Year Historical Chart." https://www.macrotrends.net/2016/10-year-treasury-bond-rate-yield-chart

[4] Ibid.

portfolio after those five years would still only be worth $715K. And that's 20 percent per year for five years in a row! What are the odds that's ever going to happen? Even if it did, you're still down almost 30 percent.

The issue is withdrawing funds from a fluctuating asset. That's why I believe many retirement plans aren't really plans at all. They are a "hope." You hope the market goes up forever and never has any setbacks. You hope that everything cooperates like inflation, taxes, interest rates, etc.

Our plans take into account taxes, inflation, all your guaranteed income sources, and potential future changes in each one. We take into account the sequence of returns risk, then, we "Stress Test" the results. We don't use averages from 1920. You need to know what happens if the market or interest rates don't cooperate. Your retirement success cannot be based on what the market will or won't make, or what interest rates will or won't be. If you can make a plan that's designed to withstand all of the negative forces you might encounter during your pre-retirement and retirement, then you have an effective plan and not a hope.

That's what makes us different.

CHAPTER 1

Longevity

You would think the prospect of the grave would loom more frightening as we age, yet many retirees say their number one fear is actually running out of money in their twilight years.[5] This fear is, unfortunately, justified, in part, because of one significant factor: We're living longer.

According to the Social Security Administration, in 1950, the average life expectancy for a sixty-five-year-old man was seventy-eight, and the average for a sixty-five-year-old woman was eighty-one. In 2021, those averages were eighty-three and eighty-eight, respectively.[6]

The bottom line of many retirees' budget woes comes down to this: They just didn't plan to live so long. Now, when we are younger and in our working years, that's not something we necessarily see as a bad thing; don't some people fantasize about living forever or, at least, reaching the ripe old age of one hundred?

However, with a longer lifespan, as we near retirement, we face a few snags. Our resources are finite—we only have so

---

5 Liz Weston. nerdwallet.com. March 25, 2021. "Will You Really Run Out of Money in Retirement?"
https://www.nerdwallet.com/article/finance/will-you-really-run-out-of-money-in-retirement
6 Social Security Administration. 2011 Trustees Report. "Actuarial Publications: Cohort Life Expectancy."
https://www.ssa.gov/OACT/TR/2011/lr5a4.html

much money to provide income—but our lifespans can be unpredictably long, perhaps longer than our resources allow. Also, longer lives don't necessarily equate with healthier lives. The longer you live, the more money you will likely need to spend on health care, even excluding long-term care needs like nursing homes.

You will also run into inflation. If you don't plan to live another twenty-five years but end up doing so, inflation at an average 3 percent will approximately double the price of goods over that time period. Put a harsh twist on that and the buying power of a ninety-year-old will be half of what they possessed if they retired at sixty-five.[7] And this is before you count the expenses of any potential health care or long-term care needs.

Because we don't necessarily get to have our cake and eat it, too, our collective increased longevity hasn't necessarily increased the healthy years of our lives. Typically, our life-extending care most widely applies to the time in our lives where we will need more care in general. Think of common situations like a pacemaker at eighty-five, or cancer treatment at seventy-eight.

"Wow, Victor," I can hear you say. "Way to start with the good news first."

I know, I've painted a grim picture, but all I'm concerned about here is cost. It's hard to put a dollar sign on life, but that is essentially what we're talking about when discussing longevity and finances. According to the Stanford Center on Longevity, more than half of pre-retirees underestimate the life expectancy of the average sixty-five-year-old.[8] Living longer isn't a bad thing; it just costs more, and one key to a sound retirement strategy is preparing for it in advance.

---

[7] Bob Sullivan, Benjamin Curry. Forbes. April 28, 2021. "Inflation And Retirement Investments: What You Need to Know." https://www.forbes.com/advisor/retirement/inflation-retirement-investments/

[8] Stanford Center on Longevity. "Underestimating Years in Retirement." http://longevity.stanford.edu/underestimating-years-in-retirement/

Example: One woman I know illustrates this picture perfectly. Her mother passed away in her late seventies after years of suffering from Alzheimer's disease. Her father died at eighty from cancer. With modern medicine and treatment, this woman survived two rounds of breast cancer, lived with diabetes, and relied on a pacemaker, extending her life to age eighty-eight, nearly a decade beyond what she anticipated. However, she and her husband had saved and planned for "just in case," trying to be prepared if they had to move, needed nursing home care, or needed to help children and grandchildren with their expenses. One of their "just-in-case" scenarios was living much longer than they anticipated. The last six years of her life were fraught with medical expenses, but she was also blessed with knowing her five great-grandchildren and deepening relationships with her children and grandchildren. She was able to pay for her own medical care, including her final two years in a nursing home, and her twilight years were truly golden.

From age eighty-five to eighty-eight, she was more socially active, with many visits from family and friends. She participated in more activities than she had in the seven years since her husband died. Her planning from decades earlier allowed her to pass on a legacy to her children when she passed away herself. The legacy she left behind can be measured both in dollar signs *and* in other intangible ways.

Living longer may be more expensive, but it can be so meaningful when you plan for your "just-in-cases."

Retiring Later

Planning for a long life in retirement partly depends on when you retire. While many people end up retiring earlier than they anticipated—due to injuries, layoffs, family crises, and other unforeseen circumstances—continuing to work past age sixty (and even sixty-five) is still a viable option for others and can be an excellent way to help establish financial comfort in retirement.

There are many reasons for this. For one, you obviously still earn a paycheck and the benefits accompanying it. Medical coverage and beefing up your retirement accounts with further savings can be significant by themselves but continuing your income also should keep you from dipping into your retirement funds, further allowing them the opportunity to grow.

Additionally, for many workers, their nine-to-five job is more than just clocking in and out. Having a sense of purpose can keep us active physically, mentally, and socially. That kind of activity and level of engagement may also help stave off many of the health problems that plague retirees. Avoiding a sedentary life is one of the advantages of staying plugged into the workforce, if possible.

One of my clients retired at his normal retirement age, but soon found himself bored and lacking purpose. He completed all his honey-do's and projects that he had put off for so long, but there was still something missing. Although he had enough funds to last a lifetime, he underestimated how important it was for him to remain engaged. He now works part-time, by choice, doing something he enjoys and is loving his "semi-retirement." He is content, knowing he doesn't need to work for financial reasons, but because he's earned the freedom to spend retirement however he chooses.

Health Care

Take a second to reflect on your health care plan. Although working up to or even past age sixty-five would allow you to avoid a coverage gap between your working years and Medicare, that may not be an option for you. Even if it is, when you retire, you will need to make some decisions about what kind of insurance coverage you may need to supplement your Medicare. Are there any medical needs you have that may require coverage in addition to Medicare? Did your parents or grandparents have any inherited medical conditions you might consider using a special savings plan to cover?

These are all questions that are important to review with your financial professional so you can be sure you have enough money put aside for health care.

In dealing with my parents, in-laws, and grandparents, I've learned the importance of having the right health coverage as you age. Sure, you get Medicare coverage from the government when you turn sixty-five. Of course, you can stay with your company coverage or spouse's plan if you're still working. The problem is that very few doctors and hospitals take Medicare by itself. For those that do, the out of pocket expenses could potentially hurt you financially if you ever need it. In my opinion, it's hard to find a good reason someone wouldn't purchase a really good supplement plan. If you can afford $100 to $200 per month, you can likely manage your health care costs throughout retirement. The Medicare Part G supplement plan pays for all the out of pocket and deductible costs on anything Medicare covers. It doesn't cover Medicare's annual deductible, which is around $200 per year and can increase with inflation. The Part F plan that also covered the annual deductible is no longer available for purchase. There are no HMOs, networks, or coinsurance. It covers you everywhere that accepts Medicare. You'll still have to purchase a prescription drug plan and possibly a dental plan, but those types of insurance typically aren't that expensive.

One of the biggest unknowns when planning for retirement can be healthcare costs. A good supplement plan allows you to manage those costs and include them into your retirement plan. You'll no longer have to be concerned about you or your spouse becoming ill and wrecking your retirement plan.

Long-Term Care

Longevity means the need for long-term care is statistically more likely to happen. If you intend to pass on a legacy, planning for long-term care is paramount, since most estimates project nearly 70 percent of Americans will need some type of it.[9] However, this may be one of the biggest, most stressful pieces of longevity planning I encounter in my work. For one thing, who wants to talk about the point in their lives when they may feel the most limited? Who wants to dwell on what will happen if they no longer can toilet, bathe, dress, or feed themselves?

I get it; this is a less-than-fun part of planning. But a little bit of preparation now can go a long way!

When it comes to your longevity, just like with your goals, one of the important things to do is sit and dream. It may not be the fun, road-trip-to-the-Grand-Canyon kind of dreaming, but you can spend time envisioning how you want your twilight years to look.

For instance, if it is important for you to live in your home for as long as possible, who will provide for the day-to-day fixes and to-dos of housework if you become ill? Will you set aside money for a service, or do you have relatives or friends nearby whom you could comfortably allow to help you? Do you prefer in-home care over a nursing home or assisted living? This could be a good time to discuss the possibility of moving into a retirement community versus staying where you are or whether it's worth moving to another state and leaving relatives behind.

These are all important factors to discuss with your spouse and children, as *now* is the right time to address questions and concerns. For instance, is aging in place more important to one spouse than the other? Are the friends or relatives who

---

[9] LongTermCare.gov. February 18, 2020. "How Much Care Will You Need?" https://acl.gov/ltc/basic-needs/how-much-care-will-you-need

live nearby emotionally, physically, and financially capable of helping you for a time if you face an illness?

Many families I meet with find these conversations very uncomfortable, particularly when children discuss nursing home care with their parents. A knee-jerk reaction for many is to promise they will care for their aging parents. This is noble and well-intentioned, but there needs to be an element of realism here. Does "help" from an adult child mean they stop by and help you with laundry, cooking, home maintenance, and bills? Or does it mean they move you into their spare room when you have hip surgery? Are they prepared to help you use the restroom and bathe if that becomes difficult for you to do on your own?

I don't mean to discourage families from caring for their own; this can be a profoundly admirable relationship when it works out. However, I've seen families put off planning for late-in-life care based on a tenuous promise that the adult children would care for their parents, only to watch as the support system crumbles. Sometimes this is because the assumed caregiver hasn't given serious thought to the preparation they would need, both in a formal sense and regarding their personal physical, emotional, and financial commitments. This is often also because we can't see the future: Alzheimer's disease and other maladies of old age can exact a heavy toll. When a loved one reaches the point where he or she is at risk of wandering away or needs help with two or more activities of daily living, it can be more than one person or family can realistically handle.

If you know what you want, communicate with your family about both the best-case and worst-case scenarios. Then, hope for the best, and plan for the worst.

Realistic Cost of Care

Wrapped up in your planning should be a consideration for the cost of long-term care. One study estimates that by 2030, the nation's long-term care costs could reach $2.5 trillion as roughly 24 million Americans require some type of long-term care.[10] The potential costs for such care and treatment can be underestimated, especially by those who have maintained robust health and find it difficult to envision future declines to their condition.

Another piece of planning for long-term care costs is anticipating inflation. It's common knowledge that prices have been and keep rising, which will lower your purchasing power on everything from food to medical care. Long-term care is a big piece of the inflation-disparity pie, which is part of why many find their estimates of nursing home care widely miss the mark. According to one survey, people expected to pay around $25,350 in annual out-of-pocket long-term care expenses, but, in reality, they'll more likely pay over $47,000.[11]

While local costs vary from state to state, here's the national median for various forms of long-term care (plus projections that account for a 3 percent annual inflation, so you can see what I'm talking about):[12]

[10] Tara O'Neill Hayes, Sara Kurtovic. Americanactionforum.org. February 18, 2020. "The Ballooning Costs of Long-Term Care." https://www.americanactionforum.org/research/the-ballooning-costs-of-long-term-care/

[11] Moll Law Group. 2021. "The Cost of Long-Term Care." https://www.molllawgroup.com/the-cost-of-long-term-care.html

[12] Genworth Financial. June 2020. "Cost of Care Survey 2020." https://www.genworth.com/aging-and-you/finances/cost-of-care.html

Long-Term Care Costs: Inflation				
	Home Health Care, Homemaker Services	Adult Day Care	Assisted Living	Nursing Home (semi-private room)
Annual 2020	$54,912	$19,236	$51,600	$93,072
Annual 2030	$73,800	$25,848	$69,348	$125,076
Annual 2040	$99,180	$34,740	$93,192	$168,096
Annual 2050	$133,284	$46,692	S125,244	$225,912

Fund Your Long-Term Care

One critical mistake I see are those who haven't planned for long-term care because they assume the government will provide everything. But that's a big misconception. The government has two health insurance programs: Medicare and Medicaid. These can greatly assist you in your health care needs in retirement but usually don't provide enough coverage to cover all your health care costs in retirement. My firm isn't a government outpost, so we don't get to make decisions when it comes to forming policy and specifics about either one of these programs. I'm going to give the overview of both, but if you want to dive into the details of these programs, you can visit www.Medicare.gov and www.Medicaid.gov.

Medicare
Medicare covers those aged sixty-five and older and those who are disabled. Medicare's coverage of any nursing-home-

related health issues is limited. It might cover your nursing home stay if it is not a "custodial" stay, and it isn't long-term. For example, if you break a bone or suffer a stroke, stay in a nursing home for rehabilitative care, and then return home, Medicare may cover you. But, if you have developed dementia or are looking to move to a nursing facility because you can no longer bathe, dress, toilet, feed yourself, or take care of your hygiene, etc., then Medicare is not going to pay for your nursing home costs.[13]

Medicaid

Medicaid is a program the states administer, so funding, protocol, and limitations vary. Compared to Medicare, Medicaid more widely covers nursing home care, but it targets a different demographic: those with low incomes.

If you have more assets than the Medicaid limit in your state and need nursing home care, you will need to use those assets to pay for your care. You will also have a list of additional state-approved ways to spend some of these assets over the Medicaid limit, such as pre-purchasing burial plots and funeral expenses or paying off debts. After that, your remaining assets fund your nursing home stay until they are gone, at which point Medicaid will jump in.

Some people aren't stymied by this, thinking they will just pass on their financial assets early, gifting them to relatives, friends, and causes so they can qualify for Medicaid when they need it. However, to prevent this exact scenario, Uncle Sam has implemented the look-back period. Currently, if you enroll in Medicaid, you are subject to having the government scrutinize the last five years of your finances for large gifts or expenses that may subject you to penalties, temporarily making you ineligible for Medicaid coverage.

So, if you're planning to preserve your money for future generations and retain control of your financial resources

---

[13] Medicare.gov. "What Part A covers." https://www.medicare.gov/what-medicare-covers/part-a/what-part-a-covers.html

during your lifetime, you'll probably want to prepare for the costs of longevity beyond a "government plan."

Self-Funding

One way to fund a longer life is the old-fashioned way, through self-funding. There are a variety of financial tools you can use, and they all have their pros and cons. If your assets are in low-interest financial vehicles (savings, bonds, CDs), you risk letting inflation erode the value of your dollar. Or, if you are relying on the stock market, you have more growth potential, but you'll also want to consider the possible implications of market volatility. What if your assets take a hit? If you suffer a loss in your retirement portfolio in early or mid-retirement, you might have the option to "tighten your belt," so to speak, and cut back on discretionary spending to allow your portfolio the room to bounce back. But, if you are retired and depend on income from a stock account that just hit a downward stride, what are you going to do?

HSAs

These days, you might also be able to self-fund through a health savings account, or HSA, if you have access to one through a high-deductible health plan (you will not qualify to save in an HSA after enrolling in Medicare). In an HSA, any growth of your tax-deductible contributions will be tax-free, and any distributions paid out for qualified health costs are also tax-free. Long-term care expenses count as health costs, so, if this is an option available to you, it is one way to use the tax advantages to self-fund your longevity. Bear in mind, if you are younger than sixty-five, any money you use for nonqualified expenses will be subject to taxes and penalties, and, if you are older than sixty-five, any HSA money you use for non-medical expenses is subject to income tax.

LTCI

One slightly more nuanced way to pay for longevity, specifically for long-term care, is long-term care insurance, or LTCI. As car insurance protects your assets in case of a car accident and home insurance protects your assets in case something happens to your house, long-term care insurance aims to protect your assets in case you need long-term care in an at-home or nursing home situation.

As with other types of insurance, you will pay a monthly or annual premium in exchange for an insurance company paying for long-term care down the road. Typically, policies cover two to three years of care, which is adequate for an "average" situation: it's estimated 70 percent of Americans will need about three years of long-term care of some kind. However, it's important to consider you might not be "average" when you are preparing for long-term care costs; on average, 20 percent of today's sixty-five-year-olds could need care for longer than five years.[14]

Now, there are a few oft-cited components of LTCI that make it unattractive for some:

- Expense — LTCI can be expensive. It is generally less expensive the younger you are, but a fifty-five-year-old couple who purchased LTCI in 2020 could expect to pay $2,080 each year for an average three-year coverage policy. And the annual cost only increases from there the older you are.[15]

- Limited options — Let's face it: LTCI may be expensive for consumers, but it can also be expensive for companies that offer it. With fewer companies willing to take on that expense, this narrows the market,

---

[14] LongTermCare.gov. February 18, 2020. "How Much Care Will You Need?" https://acl.gov/ltc/basic-needs/how-much-care-will-you-need
[15] American Association for Long-Term Care Insurance. January 12, 2021. "2021 National Long-Term Care Insurance Price Index." https://www.aaltci.org/news/long-term-care-insurance-association-news/2021-long-term-care-insurance-price-index-released-for-age-55

meaning opportunities to price shop for policies with different options or custom benefits are limited.

- If you know you need it, you might not be able to get it — Insurance companies offering LTCI are taking on a risk that you may need LTCI. That risk is the foundation of the product—you may or may not need it. If you know you will need it because you have a dementia diagnosis or another illness for which you will need long-term care, you will likely not qualify for LTCI coverage.

- Use it or lose it—If you have LTCI and are in the minority of Americans who die having never needed long-term care, all the money you paid into your LTCI policy is gone.

- Possibly fluctuating rates—Your rate is not locked in on LTCI. Companies maintain the ability to raise or lower your premium amounts. This means some seniors face an ultimatum: Keep funding a policy at what might be a less affordable rate *or* lose coverage and let go of all the money they paid in so far.

After that, you might be thinking, "How can people possibly be interested in LTCI?" But let me repeat myself—as many as 70 percent of Americans will need long-term care. And, although only 8 percent of Americans have purchased LTCI, keep in mind the high cost of nursing home care. Can you afford $7,000 a month to put into nursing home care and still have enough left over to protect your legacy? This is a very real concern: One study says 72 percent of Americans are impoverished by the end of just one year in a nursing home.[16] So, not to sound like a broken record, but it is vitally

---

[16] Kate Dore. CNBC. Aug. 26, 2021. "Most retirees will need long-term care. These are the best ways to pay for it." https://www.cnbc.com/2021/08/26/most-retirees-will-need-long-term-care-these-are-ways-to-pay-for-it-.html

important to have a plan in place to deal with longevity and long-term care if you intend to leave a financial legacy.

We previously offered traditional long-term care policies when they were more affordable. You could get a lifetime benefit for a pretty small premium. With rising medical costs and increased longevity, the insurance companies started hemorrhaging cash from these early policies. Now, health care coverage costs more than ever, with more increases expected in the near future.[17] If that is a potential issue in your retirement plan, you may want to consider covering all or part of the cost of long-term care through different annuity or life insurance policies with health care riders.

Product Riders

LTCI and self-funding are not the only ways to plan for the expenses of longevity. Some companies are getting creative with their products, particularly insurance companies. One way they are retooling to meet people's needs is through optional product riders on annuities and life insurance. Elsewhere in this book, I talk about annuity basics, but here's a brief overview: Annuities are insurance contracts. You pay the insurance company a premium, either as a lump sum or as a series of payments over a set amount of time, in exchange for guaranteed income payments. One of the advantages of an annuity is it has access to riders, which allow you to tweak your contract for a fee, usually about 1 percent of the contract value annually. One annuity rider some companies offer is a long-term care rider. If you have an annuity with a long-term care rider and are not in need of long-term care, your contract behaves as any annuity contract would—nothing changes. Generally speaking, if you reach a point when you can't perform multiple functions of daily life on your own, you

---

[17] Amy Stulick. Skilled Nursing News. Sept. 20, 2021. "Long-Term Care Costs Expected to Further Increase by 5% in Next Six Months." https://skillednursingnews.com/2021/09/long-term-care-costs-expected-to-further-increase-by-5-in-next-six-months/

notify the insurance company, and a representative will turn on those provisions of your contract.

Like LTCI, different companies and products offer different options. Some annuity long-term care riders offer coverage of two years in a nursing home situation. Others cap expenses at two times the original annuity's value. It greatly depends. Some people prefer this option because there isn't a "use-it-or-lose-it" piece; if you die without ever having needed long-term care, you still will have had the income benefit from the base contract. Still, as with any annuities or insurance contracts, there are the usual restrictions and limitations. Withdrawing money from the contract will affect future income payments, early distributions can result in a penalty, income taxes may apply, and, because the insurance company's solvency is what guarantees your payments, it's important to do your research about the insurance company you are considering purchasing a contract from.

Understandably, a discussion on long-term care is bound to feel at least a little tedious. Yet, this is a critical piece of planning for income in retirement, particularly if you want to leave a legacy.

A close friend of mine thought he had long-term care all figured out. He didn't have a lot of assets, probably around $500K, and he expected to spend down most of his assets before he would need long-term care. If the time came that he needed to move into a facility, his plan was to gift any remaining assets to his children so that he'd qualify for Medicare and his stay would be paid for.

The problem is he contracted an illness in his seventies, while his wife was still in perfect health. He didn't realize that gifting your assets to your children when you need long-term care wouldn't work, because the government looks back five years to ensure nothing like that occurred.

He also didn't realize how much of his assets needed to be spent down to qualify for Medicare, leaving his wife penniless. Nicer facilities have very few Medicaid beds, if any, which makes long-term stays very costly. His wife is now spending her golden years scraping by to pay for the facility, knowing there will be a point where she'll probably lose her independence and have to move in with her children.

Spousal Planning

Here's one thing to keep in mind no matter how you plan to save: Many of us will be planning for more than ourselves. Look back at all the stats on health events and the likelihood of long life and long-term care. If they hold true for a single individual, then the likelihood of having a costly health or long-term care event is even higher for a married couple. You'll be planning for not just one life, but two. So, when it comes to long-term care insurance, annuities, self-funding, or whatever strategy you are looking at using, be sure you are funding longevity for the both of you.

It is extremely important to consider both spouses when planning. A widow and her two children came to me after their father passed away. After carefully looking over their assets, I discovered the father split all of the family's assets into three parts, giving his wife and children one-third each. They explained it was very important for their father to leave a legacy.

The only issue was the mother didn't receive enough to maintain her lifestyle, which was far from extravagant. The children were not willing to give the funds back to their mother. Their feelings were that the mother would mismanage the funds and that it was very important to their father that they receive equal funds. They explained that if something happened to their mother, they would take care of her. This is not as uncommon as you might think. The mother had some other issues, and within a few weeks, she committed suicide.

I'm not sharing this story to make anyone sad or angry at the children, or even at the father. I'm sure he had the best intentions for his family, and that the children had the best intentions for their mother. The biggest issue is that the father didn't plan properly to ensure that his wife of forty years was taken care of if he passed away. If he would have done some simple retirement planning, the issue could have been avoided.

Remember, when you're on a plane, the flight attendants tell you to don your oxygen mask first, and then put them on your children. I have seven children, and I told them, "Kids, you're welcome to every dime your mother and I don't spend. If there's anything left over, you're welcome to it. Hopefully, I'll plan well enough, so I don't have to live with one of you. Trust me, I'm sure I won't be the most pleasant eighty-year-old you've ever met."

Of course, I want my children to receive some kind of legacy, but it's more important for my kids to know that I love their mother enough to ensure she never has to worry about finances if I pass away. There is so much sadness, loneliness, and sometimes chaos when a loved one passes that the last thing I want my loved one to experience is financial hardship. It's hard enough when there are no financial issues.

Always think about two lives instead of just your own. You must run several scenarios that see how your finances handle the death or incapacity of a spouse. Don't assume the stock market or real estate market will go up forever in your planning. Plan for the worst and hope for the best. Improper planning is one of the most crucial, yet avoidable, mistakes I have seen in my thirty-five years of retirement planning.

CHAPTER 2
Market Volatility

Up and down. Roller coaster. Merry-go-round. Bulls and bears. Peak-to-trough.

Sound familiar? This is the language we use to talk about the stock market. With volatility and spikes, even our language is jarring, bracing, and vivid.

Still, financial strategies tend to revolve around market-based products, for good reasons. For one thing, there is no other financial class that packs the same potential for growth, pound for pound, as stock-based products. Because of growth potential, inflation protection, and new opportunities, it may be unwise to avoid the market entirely.

However, along with the potential for growth is the potential for loss. Many of the people I see in my office come in still feeling a bit burned from the market drama of 2000 to 2010. That was a rough stretch, and many of us are once-bitten-twice-shy investors, right?

So how do we balance these factors? How do we try to satisfy both the need for protection and the need for growth?

For one thing, it is important to recognize the value of diversity. Now, I'm not just talking about the diversity of assets among different kinds of stocks, or even different kinds of stocks and bonds. That's only one kind of diversity; while important, both stocks and bonds, though different, are both still market-based products. Most market-based products, even within a diverse portfolio, tend to rise or lower as a whole, just like an incoming tide. Therefore, a portfolio diverse in only market-sourced products won't automatically protect your assets during times when the market declines.

In addition to the sort of "horizontal diversity" you have by purchasing a variety of stocks and bonds from different companies, I encourage having "vertical diversity," or diversity among asset classes. This means having different product types, including securities products, bank products, and insurance products—with varying levels of growth potential, liquidity, and protection—all in accordance with your unique situation, goals, and needs.

Before anything is recommended to our clients, their information is inputted into a comprehensive retirement planning software. Information like Social Security benefits, pension, rental income, miscellaneous income, assets, liabilities, expenses, life insurance, etc.

After everything is accounted for, we stress test the results. What if the market or interest rates don't cooperate? What if inflation or taxes increase? What if one spouse needs long-term care? What if one spouse passes away?

Then, and only then, can you see if changing or adding stocks, bonds, life insurance, annuities, or other financial tools might make sense. It's always amazed me that some "financial advisors" can make a recommendation of a managed stock account or an annuity without taking all of these factors into consideration. There is absolutely nothing wrong with a "do it yourself" approach to financial or retirement planning. The only issue is that you've only experienced one person's finances: your own. You don't know what you don't know.

There are so many issues that an individual not specifically trained in planning for a large number of people may not know to account for in their own planning. There's a lot more to retirement planning than picking the right stocks, bonds, or annuities. What's most important is determining how each tool fits into your unique financial circumstances.

One of the biggest mistakes I see people making is taking financial advice from a friend, relative, or colleague. Their perspective is, "This person is more successful than I am, so their advice must be better than mine or even a financial professional's."

Let's be honest, no one would take financial advice from their broke uncle. Now, if you have a friend who's very wealthy or you consider them more wealthy of knowledgeable than you, of course, you might take that advice. The problem is your friend's financial situation and circumstances might be completely different than yours. A really good portfolio allocation for them could be detrimental to your situation.

I've seen circumstances where a friend of a couple that was very well off took their advice on how to invest, and it didn't work out as planned. What they didn't realize is the friend who gave them the advice came from a wealthy family. The couple was given a large sum of money from their parents when their children were younger. They also didn't realize their parents (the children's grandparents) paid for the kids' college expenses. This allowed them at a young age to pay off their home and save much more than average. This couple giving them the advice didn't have the expenses or worries that a normal couple raising children would face. They were also set to inherit a lot of money regardless of how risky their investment portfolio might be.

Just because a person appears more successful than you, even if they're in a similar occupation. Doesn't mean they're any more saavy than you or anyone else at managing their finances. A professional can help you in more ways than you could imagine.

The Color of Money

When you're looking at the overall diversity of your portfolio, part of the equation is knowing which products fit in what category: what has liquidity, what has protection, and what has growth potential.

Before we dive in, keep in mind these aren't absolutes. You might think of liquidity, growth, and protection as primary colors. While some products will look pretty much yellow, red, or blue, others will have a mix of characteristics, making them more green, orange, or purple.

Growth

I like to think of the growth category as red. It's powerful, it's somewhat volatile, and it's also the category where we have the greatest opportunities for growth and loss. Often, products in the growth category will have a good deal of liquidity but very little protection. These are our market-based products and strategies, and we think of them mostly in shades of red and orange, to designate their growth and liquidity. This is a good place to be when you're young—think fast cars and flashy leather jackets—but its allure often wanes as you move closer to retirement. Examples of "red" products include:

- Stocks
- Equities
- Exchange-traded funds
- Mutual funds
- Corporate bonds
- Real estate investment trusts
- Speculations
- Alternative investments

Liquidity

Yellow is my liquid category color. I typically recommend having at least enough yellow money to cover six months' to two year's worth of expenses in case of emergency. Yellow assets don't need a lot of growth potential; they just need to be readily available when we need them. The "yellow" category includes assets like:

- Cash

- Money market accounts

Protection

The color of protection, to me, is blue. Tranquil, peaceful, sure, even if it lacks a certain amount of flash. This is the direction I like to see people generally move toward as they're nearing retirement. The red, flashy look of stock market returns and the risk of possible overnight losses is less attractive as we near retirement and look for more consistency and reliability. While this category doesn't come with a lot of liquidity, the products here are backed by an insurance company, a bank, or a government entity. "Blue" products include things such as:
- Certificates of deposit (backed by banks)
- Government-based bonds (backed by the U.S. government)
- Life insurance (backed by insurance companies)
- Annuities (backed by insurance companies)

The stock market has produced the greatest gains of any kind of investment over the long term. No other investment has proven to beat inflation long term more than stocks. Although, there is no guarantee that it will perform like this in the future. With that being said, does it make sense for a seventy-year-old to be 90 percent invested in stocks? Most likely not. A balanced portfolio of growth and protection is key to long-term success.

401(k)s

I want to take a second to specifically address a product many retirees will be using to build their retirement income: the 401(k) and other retirement accounts. Any of these retirement accounts (IRAs, 401(k)s, 403(b)s, etc.) are basically "tax wrappers." What do I mean by that? Well, depending on your plan provider, a 401(k) could include target-date funds, passively managed products, stocks, bonds, mutual funds, or even variable, fixed, and fixed index annuities, all collected in one place and governed by rules (a.k.a. the "tax wrapper"). These rules govern how much money you can put inside, what ways you can put it in, when you will pay taxes on it, and when you can take the money out. Inside the 401(k), each of the products inside the "tax wrapper" might have its own fees or commissions, in addition to the management fee you pay on the 401(k) itself.

Now, fees can be troublesome. You can't get something for nothing, and fees are how many financial companies and professionals make a living. Yet, it's important to recognize even a fee of a single percentage point is money out of your pocket—money that represents not just the one-time fee of today but also represents an opportunity cost. One study found a single percentage point fee could cost a millennial close to $600,000 over forty years of saving.[18] For someone closer to retirement, how much do you think fees may have cost over their lifetime?

Even for those close to retirement, it's important to look at management fees and assess if you think you're getting what you pay for. Over the course of ten years, those puppies can add up, and you may have decades ahead of you in which you will need to rely on your assets.

Dollar-Cost Averaging

With 401(k)s and other market-based retirement products, when you are investing for the long term, dollar-cost averaging is a concept that can work in your favor. When the market is trending up, if you are consistently paying in money,

---

[18] Dayana Yochim and Jonathan Todd. NerdWallet. "How a 1% Fee Could Cost Millennials $590,000 in Retirement Savings." https://www.nerdwallet.com/blog/investing/millennial-retirement-fees-one-percent-half-million-savings-impact/

month over month, great; your investments can grow, and you are adding to your assets. When the market takes a dip, no problem; your dollars buy more shares at a lower price. At some point, we hope the market will rebound, in which case your shares can grow and possibly be more valuable than they were before. This concept is what we call "dollar-cost averaging." While it can't ensure a profit or guarantee against losses, it's a time-tested strategy for investing in a volatile market.

However, when you are in retirement, this strategy may work against you. You may have heard of "reverse" dollar-cost averaging. Before, when the market lost ground, you were "bargain-shopping"; your dollars purchased more assets at a reduced price. When you are in retirement, you are no longer the purchaser; you are selling. So, in a down market, you have to sell more assets to make the same amount of money as what you made in a favorable market.

I've had lots of people step into my office to talk to me about this, emphasizing "my advisor says the market always bounces back, and I have to just hold on for the long term."

There's some basis for this thinking; thus far, the market has always rebounded to higher heights than before. But this is no guarantee, and the prospect of potentially higher returns in five years may not be very helpful in retirement if you are relying on the income from those returns to pay this month's electric bill, for example.

Market volatility is addressed through a well-thought-out process. Carefully crafting a portfolio allocation with the right balance of risk and protection is crucial. The right balance of income and growth.

Paying expenses from a fluctuating asset like stocks is never a good idea. It doesn't matter if they're growth or dividend stocks. I strongly believe expenses should always be paid from a guaranteed income source. Your electric bill or mortgage can't be reliant on whether the stock market makes money or not. Examples of a guaranteed income source would be certificates of deposit (CDs), bonds, or annuities. Otherwise, your retirement dreams might be affected from the "sequence of returns" risk.

If you experience market losses in the first few years of retirement, you run the real risk of portfolio exhaustion, regardless of what the market's long-term return would indicate. The math proves it and math never lies. Having the right pieces in place can make all the difference in the world.

Is There a "Perfect" Product?

To bring us back around to the discussion of protection, growth, and liquidity, the ideal product would be a "ten" in all three categories, right? Completely guaranteed, doubling in size every few years, and accessible whenever you want. Does such a product exist? Anyone who says, "yes" is either ignorant or malevolent.

Instead of running in circles looking for that perfect product, the silver bullet, the unicorn of financial strategies, it's more important to circle back to the concept of a balanced, asset-diverse portfolio.

This is why your interests may be best served when you work with a trusted financial professional who knows what various financial products can do and how to use them in your personal retirement plan.

There is no perfect investment. Stocks have market risk. Bonds have default and interest rate risk. Annuities sometimes have long terms subject to early withdrawal charges. You always have the risk that inflation will outperform your investments. CDs have default risk over the limits and penalties, and they might not keep up with inflation. When economic conditions change, you must be able to adapt. Here's an example: Let's look at a typical 50/50 portfolio (50 percent allocated to stocks and 50 percent allocated to bonds). When interest rates are extremely low, you run the real risk of half of your portfolio earning much less than inflation. This often leads to people having a much higher equity allocation than they should, which makes their portfolios riskier. You have to think outside the box.

This also leads some to use alternatives like dividend stocks or even, sometimes, blue chip stocks as part of their fixed income allocation. This can put the entire portfolio at a higher risk of loss, when you should be looking for a balanced portfolio.

At the writing of this book, 10-year Treasuries have been floating between 1.00 to 1.5 percent[19] and inflation has risen to 5 or 6 percent.[20] Five-year CDs are averaging around 1 percent.[21] As you can see, there is a real risk of losing purchasing power staying with the more traditional approaches to portfolio allocation.

At the same time, 5-year multi-year guaranteed annuities (MYGAs) are paying around 3 percent per year.[22] It's not perfect when there are spikes in inflation, but it is two to three times more interest than Treasuries and CDs. For some willing to risk potential interest, but still have principal guaranteed, there are some good potential bond alternatives, like fixed index annuities (FIAs).

---

[19] Multpl.com. Dec. 29, 2021. "10 Year Treasury Rate by Month." https://www.multpl.com/10-year-treasury-rate/table/by-month

[20] U.S. Inflation Calculator. December 2021. "Current US Inflation Rates: 2000-2021." https://www.usinflationcalculator.com/inflation/current-inflation-rates/

[21] Matthew Goldman. Bankrate. Dec. 16, 2021. "Best 5-year CD rates." https://www.bankrate.com/banking/cds/best-5-year-cd-rates/

[22] All Things Annuity. December 2021. "Current 5 Year Annuity Rates." https://www.allthingsannuity.com/rates/05-year-fixed-annuity-rates.htm

CHAPTER 3

Annuities

I n my practice, I offer my clients a variety of products—
from securities to insurance—all designed to help them
reach their financial goals. You may be wondering: Why
single out a single product in this book?

Well, while most of my clients have a pretty good
understanding of business and finance, I sometimes find those
who have the impression there must be magic involved. Some
people assume there is a magic finance wand we can wave to
change years' worth of savings into a strategy for retirement
income. But it's not as easy as a goose laying golden eggs or
the Fairy Godmother turning a pumpkin into a coach!

Finances aren't magic; it takes lots of hard work and,
typically, several financial products and strategies to pull
together a complete retirement plan. Of all the financial
products I work with, it seems people find none more
mysterious than annuities. And, if I may say, even some of
those who recognize the word "annuity" have a limited
understanding of the product. So, in the interest of
demystifying annuities, let me tell you a little about what an
annuity is.

In general, insurance is a financial hedge against risk. Car
owners buy auto insurance to protect their finances in case
they injure someone or someone injures them. Homeowners
have house insurance to protect their finances in case of a fire,
flood, or another disaster. People have life insurance to

protect their finances in case of untimely death. Almost juxtaposed to life insurance, people have annuities in case of a long life; annuities can give you financial protection by providing consistent and reliable income payments.

The basic premise of an annuity is you, the annuitant, pay an insurance company some amount in exchange for their contractual guarantee they will pay you income for a certain time period. How that company pays you, for how long, and how much they offer are all determined by the annuity contract you enter into with the insurance company.

How You Get Paid

There are two ways for an annuity contract to provide income: The first is through what is called annuitization, and the second is through the use of income riders. We'll get into income riders in a bit, but let's talk about annuitization. That nice, long word is, in my opinion, one reason annuities have a reputation for mystery and misinformation.

Annuitization

When someone "annuitizes" a contract, it is the point where he or she turns on the income stream. Once a contract has been annuitized, there is no going back. With annuities, if the policyholder lives longer than the insurance company planned, the insurance company is still obligated to pay him or her, even if the payments end up being way more than the contract's actual value. If, however, the policyholder dies an untimely death, depending on the contract type, the insurance company may keep anything left of the money that funded the annuity—nothing would be paid out to the contract holder's survivors. You see where that could make some people balk? Now, modern annuities rarely rely on annuitization for the income portion of the contract, and instead have so many bells and whistles that the old concept of annuitization seems outdated, but because this is still an option, it's important to at least understand the basic concept.

Riders

Speaking of bells and whistles, let's talk about riders. Modern annuities have a lot of different options these days, many in the form of riders you can add to your contract for a fee—usually about 1 percent of the contract value per year. Each rider has its particulars, and the types of riders available will vary by the type of annuity contract purchased, but I'll just briefly outline some of these little extras:

- Lifetime income rider: Contract guarantees you an enhanced income for life
- Death benefit rider: Contract pays an enhanced death benefit to your beneficiaries even if you have annuitized
- Return of premium rider: Guarantees you (or your beneficiaries) will at least receive back the premium value of the annuity
- Long-term care rider: Provides a certain amount, sometimes as much as twice the principal value of the contract, to help pay for long-term care if the contract holder is moved to a nursing home or assisted living situation

This isn't an extensive look, and usually the riders have fancier names based on the issuing company, like "Lorem Ipsum Insurance Company Income Preferred Bonus Fixed Index Annuity rider," but I just wanted to show you what some of the general options are in layperson's terms.

Types of Annuities

Annuities break down into four basic types: immediate, variable, fixed, and fixed index.

Immediate

Immediate annuities primarily rely on annuitization to provide income—you give the insurance company a lump sum up front, and your payments begin immediately. Once you begin receiving income payments, the transaction is irreversible, and you no longer have access to your money in a lump sum. When you die, any remaining contract value is typically forfeited to the insurance company.

All other annuity contract types are "deferred" contracts, meaning you fund your policy as a lump sum or over a period of years and you give it the opportunity to grow over time—sometimes years, sometimes decades.

Variable

A variable annuity is an insurance contract as well as an investment. It's sold by insurance companies, but only through someone who is registered to sell investment products. With a variable annuity contract, the insurance company invests your premiums in subaccounts that are tied to the stock market. This makes it a bit different from the other annuity contract types because it is the only contract where your money is subject to losses because of market declines. Your contract value has a greater opportunity to grow, but it also stands to lose. Additionally, your contract's value will be subject to the underlying investment's fees and limitations—including capital gains taxes, management fees, etc. Once it is time for you to receive income from the contract, the insurance company will pay you a certain income, locked in at whatever your contract's value was.

In general, the expenses of retail variable annuities (VAs) are too high for me to recommend them to my clients. When you add the mortality and expense charges, fund fees, marketing fees, and rider fees, I've seen VA total fees eclipse 5 percent per year. Now, 5 percent fees definitely benefit one side of the table, but not necessarily the consumer. I was the

President of a Broker-Dealer for decades who could sell VAs, but chose not to. There is no denying there are benefits to VAs, but the benefits don't justify the expenses, in my opinion. There are some decent low-cost VAs, but they don't offer most of the living benefits so sought after by consumers. I have found too many low-cost alternatives to recommend a VA. If you're in the market for something tax deferred and you don't need the living benefit riders, the low cost VA might be an option.

Fixed

A traditional fixed annuity is pretty straightforward. You purchase a contract with a guaranteed interest rate and, when you are ready, the insurance company will make regular income payments to you at whatever payout rate your contract guarantees. Those payments will continue for the rest of your life and, if you choose, for the remainder of your spouse's life.

Fixed annuities don't have much in the way of upside potential, but many people like them for their guarantees (after all, if your Aunt May lives to be ninety-five, knowing she has a paycheck later in life can be her mental and financial safety net), as well as for their predictability. Unlike variable annuities, which are subject to market risk and might be up one year and down the next, you can easily calculate the value of your fixed annuity over your lifetime.

Fixed Index

To recap, variable annuities take on more risk to offer more possibilities to grow. Fixed annuities have less potential growth, but they protect your principal. In the last couple of decades, many insurance companies have retooled their product line to offer fixed index annuities, which are sort of midway between variable and fixed annuities on that risk/reward spectrum. Fixed index annuities offer greater growth potential than traditional fixed annuities but less than variable annuities. Like traditional fixed annuities, however, fixed index annuities are protected from downside market losses.

Fixed index annuities earn interest that is tied to the market, meaning that, instead of your contract value growing at a set interest rate like a traditional fixed annuity, it has the potential to grow within a range. Your contract's value is credited interest based on the performance of an external market index like the S&P 500 while never being invested in the market itself. You can't invest in the S&P 500 directly, but each year, your annuity as the potential to earn interest based on the chosen index's performance, submit to limits set by the company such as caps, spreads and participation rates. For instance, if your contract caps your interest at 5 percent, then in a year that the S&P 500 gains 3 percent, your annuity value increases 3 percent. If the S&P 500 gains 35 percent, your annuity value gets a 5 percent interest bump. But since your money isn't actually invested in the market with a fixed index annuity, if the market nosedives (such as happened during 2000, 2008 and 2020, anyone?) you won't see any increase in your contract value. Conversely, there will also be no decrease in your contract value—no matter how badly the market performed, as long as you follow the terms of the contract, you won't lose any of the interest you were credited in previous years.

So, what if the S&P 500 shows a market loss of 30 percent? Your contract value isn't going anywhere (unless you purchased an optional rider—this charge will still come out of your annuity value each year). For those who are more interested in protection than growth potential, fixed index annuities can be an attractive option because, when the stock market has a long period of positive performance, a fixed index annuity can enjoy conservative growth. And, during stretches where the stock market is erratic and stock values across the board take significant losses? Fixed index annuities won't lose anything due to the stock market volatility.

There are times when considering a fixed index annuity (FIA) might make sense:

1. If you would like your funds protected with your principal guaranteed, but aren't satisfied with returns on traditional fixed income like bonds or CDs. FIAs give you more upside potential without the downside risk, although the growth is not guaranteed, and you could earn 0 percent in some years

2. If you'd like to protect a portion of your assets from judgments, want to defer taxes, and would like the potential for higher interest.

3. If you would like a guaranteed income stream. Let's say you aren't interested in annuitization or losing control of those assets. An FIA with an optional life income rider guarantees income for the rest of your life, the balance has the opportunity to grow while you're receiving the income stream, and you have the option for your heirs to receive the balance if you pass.

Annuities with lifetime income riders can often provide more "income per dollar" if you defer the income for a few years. Getting more income per dollar can make sense in two ways. When you put your money into buckets (reserve cash, growth, income, etc.), the most restrictive bucket will usually be your income bucket. This is money that needs to pay the bills for the rest of your life. If you can get more income per dollar from a specific portion of your portfolio, that means you can have a lower amount allocated to the most restrictive bucket. The second reason is that many people's main objective is to receive the most income from their savings. Leaving a legacy isn't usually as important and getting the most income. By deferring an FIA life income rider a few years, the income is potentially much higher than you could receive in any other income producing investment and it's guaranteed to never run out.

Consumers like the flexibility, growth potential, and guaranteed income fixed index annuities can provide. Be sure and read the fine print and think carefully before considering lower-rated carriers. FIAs have historically been protected, but it's hard to argue staying with companies that have been around a long time and maintain a strong financial track record.

Keep in mind, annuities do involve limitations, fees, and expenses, as well as a time commitment before you can withdraw a significant portion of your money without a penalty.

Other Things to Know About Annuities

We just talked about the four kinds of annuity contracts available, but all of them have some commonalities as annuities.

For all annuities, the contractual guarantees are only as strong as the insurance company that sells the product, which makes it important to thoroughly check the credit ratings of any company whose products you are considering.

Annuities are tax-deferred, meaning you don't have to pay taxes on interest earnings each year as the contract value grows. Instead, you will pay ordinary income taxes on your withdrawals. These are meant to be long-term products, so, like other tax-deferred or tax-advantaged products, if you begin taking withdrawals from your contract before age fifty-nine-and-one-half, you may also have to pay a 10 percent federal tax penalty. Also, while annuities are generally considered illiquid, most contracts allow you to withdraw up to 10 percent of your contract value every year. Withdraw any more, however, and you could incur additional surrender penalties.

Keep in mind, your withdrawals will deplete the accumulated cash value, death benefit, and, possibly, the rider values of your contract.

Annuities are just a tool, like stocks, bonds, CDs, etc. They can be an attractive option for retirement savings depending on the objective and risk tolerance of the individual person. They aren't for everyone, but might be a really good option for the right person.

Here are a few examples of when an annuity might be a good option to consider:

1. Let's say you're a fifty-seven-year-old couple who wants to retire in ten years when you're both sixty-seven. Your portfolio is about $1 million. Let's say you've run the numbers and believe you'll need $50K in income from your $1 million portfolio to supplement Social Security. You could put $500,000 in a fixed index annuity that would guarantee you and your spouse approximately $50,000 per year for both of your lives, leaving the remaining $500,000 to potentially grow. That way, no matter what happens to the market or interest rates, your lifestyle will be secured for the rest of your life. In contrast, if you take the same $1 million and put it in 2 percent bonds, you're looking at $20,000 per year. Even if you assume the portfolio will grow to $2 million by the time the couple retires, the income would be approximately $40,000 per year (assuming the bonds remained constant at 2 percent every year). Maybe interest rates are higher and they could secure more income. Maybe they're lower. This is a product for someone seeing income guarantees without annuitization. You could take the proceeds and put them into an immediate annuity, but you lose control of the funds, the balance wouldn't earn interest, and your heirs might not receive anything if you both passed away prematurely. That is why the fixed index annuity with the life income rider might make more sense. Also, some FIA income riders have a long-term care rider that would could potentially double the income payment for a number of years (usually three to five years) to help pay for long-term care if one of you needed it.

2. Let's use the same fifty-seven-year-old couple plans on retiring in ten years with a current portfolio of $1 million. Let's assume they have low expenses that should be sufficiently paid for with Social Security and rental income. They want their money protected without any market risk. Current bond and CD rates aren't attractive to them. They could purchase a fixed index annuity without an income rider that is specifically designed for protected growth potential. A fixed index annuity will give them the protection they seek, with interest rates tied to the movement of external indexes while never being invested in the market itself. Any interest earned is then locked in and guaranteed, along with their principal.

3. A consumer who is seeking a protected vehicle, but is not interested in current rates for traditional fixed income like CDs or bonds. A multi-year guaranteed annuity (MYGA) is a very simple type of annuity that guarantees a specific interest rate for one to ten years. Rates may be higher than bonds or CDs. All annuities are tax deferred, too, so you don't pay taxes on any interest until withdrawn, unlike bank CDs or bonds.

Annuities aren't for everyone, but it's important to understand them before saying "yea" or "nay" on whether they fit into your plan; otherwise, you're not operating with complete information, wouldn't you agree? Regardless, you should talk to a financial professional who can help you understand annuities, help you dissect your particular financial needs, and help show you whether an annuity is appropriate for your retirement income plan.

CHAPTER 4
Retirement Income

Retirement. For many of us, it's what we've saved for and dreamed of, pinning our hopes to a magical someday. Is that someday full of traveling? Is it filled with grandkids? Gardening? Maybe your fondest dream is simply never having to work again, never having to clock in or be accountable to someone else.

Your ability to do these things all hinges on *income*. Without the money to support these dreams, even a basic level of work-free lifestyle is unsustainable. That's why planning for your income in retirement is so foundational. But where do we begin?

It's easy to feel overwhelmed by this question. Some may feel the urge to amass a large lump sum and then try to put it all in one product—insurance, investments, liquid assets—to provide all the growth, liquidity, and income they need. Instead, I think you need a more balanced approach. After all, retirement planning isn't magic. Like I mention elsewhere, there is no single product that can be all things to all people (or even all things to one person). No approach works unilaterally for everyone. That's why it's important to talk to a financial professional who can help you lay down the basics and take you step-by-step through the process. Not only will you have the assurance you have addressed the areas you need to, but you will also have an ally who can help you break down the process and help keep you from feeling overwhelmed.

Sources of Income

Thinking of all the pieces of your retirement expenses might be intimidating. But, like cleaning out a junk drawer or revisiting that garage remodel, once you have laid everything out, you can begin to sort things into categories.

Once you have a good overall picture of where your expenses will lie, you can start stacking up the resources to cover them.

Social Security

Social Security is a guaranteed, inflation-protected federal insurance program playing a significant part in most of our retirement plans. From delaying until you've reached full retirement age or beyond to examining spousal benefits, as I discuss elsewhere in this book, there is plenty you can do to try to make the most of this monthly benefit. As with all your retirement income sources, it's important to consider how to make this resource stretch to provide the most bang and buck for your situation.

Pension

Another generally reliable source of retirement income for you might be a pension, if you are one of the lucky people who still has one.

If you don't have a pension, go ahead and skim on to the next section. If you do have a pension, keep on reading.

Because your pension can be such a central piece of your retirement income plan, you will want to put some thought into answering basic questions about it.

How well is your pension funded? Since the heyday of the pension plan, companies and governments have neglected to fund their pension obligations, causing a persistent problem with this otherwise reliable asset. Public pensions face a collective $4.998 trillion deficit, according to the U.S. Pension Tracker.[23] The Public Benefit Guaranty Association, which helps insure private pensions, reports there is a $63.7 billion shortfall in multiemployer plans, affecting half of all multiemployer plans.[24] If you have a pension, it is quite possibly included in those statistics.

In addition to checking up on your pension's health, check into what your options are for withdrawing your pension. If you have already retired and made those decisions, this may be a foregone conclusion. If not, it pays to know what you can expect and what decisions you can make, such as taking spousal options to cover your husband or wife if he or she outlives you.

Also, some companies are incentivizing lump-sum payouts of pensions to reduce the companies' payment liabilities. If that's the case with your employer, talk to your financial professional to see if it might be prudent to do something like that or if it might be better to stick with lifetime payments or other options.

Your 401(k) and IRA

One "modern way" to save for retirement is in a 401(k) or IRA (or their nonprofit or governmental equivalents). These tax-advantaged accounts are, in my opinion, a poor substitute for pensions, but one of the biggest disservices we do to ourselves is to not take full advantage of them in the first place. According to one article, only 32 percent of Americans invest in a 401(k), though 59 percent of employed Americans have access to a 401(k) benefit option.[25]

[23] U.S. Pension Tracker. April 2021. us.pensiontracker.org

[24] Pension Benefit Guaranty Corporation. December 10, 2020. "Deficit FAQs." https://www.pbgc.gov/about/faq/pg/deficit-faqs

[25] Amin Dabit. personalcapital.com. April 1, 2021. "The Average 401k Balance by Age." https://www.personalcapital.com/blog/retirement-planning/average-401k-balance-age/

Also, if you have changed jobs over the years, do the work of tracking down any benefits from your past employers. You might have an IRA here or a 401(k) there; keep track of those so you can pull them together and look at those assets when you're ready to look at establishing sources of retirement income.

Do You Have...

- Life insurance?
- Annuities?
- Long-term care insurance?
- Any passive income sources?
- Stock and bond portfolios?
- Liquid assets? (What's in your bank account?)
- Alternative investments?
- Rental properties?

It's important, if you are going through the work of sitting with a financial professional, to look at your full retirement income picture and pull together *all* your assets, no matter how big or small. From the free insurance policy offered at your bank to the sizable investment in your brother-in-law's modestly successful furniture store, you want to have a good idea of where your money is.

I have a client who had several accounts they really hadn't looked at for years. The accounts were mainly old 401(k)s from previous companies and a few small brokerage accounts. They have a successful business and never really paid attention to these old accounts. To their surprise when everything was put together, these accounts added up into over $1 million. Just taking the required minimum distributions (RMDs) from the retirement accounts amounted to a sizable annual income. Obviously, they were pleasantly surprised by the total. They were even more surprised that these accounts could actually pay a significant portion of their retirement expenses.

It's always a good idea to keep a decent spreadsheet of your assets and update it as much as possible. Most stories don't go as well as this couple's. More often than not, people think they have more or think the income their portfolio should generate is higher than probable or possible.

Retirement Income Needs

How much income will you need in retirement? How do you determine that? A lot of people work toward a random number, thinking, "If I can just have a million dollars, I'll be comfortable in retirement!" Don't get me wrong; it is possible to save up a lot of money and then retire in the hopes you can keep your monthly expenses lower than some set estimation. But I think this carries a general risk of running out of money. Instead, I work with my clients to find out what their current and projected income needs are and then work from there to see how we might cover any gaps between what they have and what they want.

Goals and Dreams

I like to start with your pie in the sky. Do you find yourself planning for your vacations more thoroughly than you do your retirement? It's not uncommon for Americans to spend more time planning our vacations than we spend planning our retirements. Maybe it's because planning a vacation is less stressful: Having a week at the beach go awry is, well, a walk on the beach compared to running out of money in retirement. Whatever the case, perhaps it would be better if you thought of your retirement as a vacation in and of itself—no clocking in, no boss, no overtime. If you felt unlimited by financial strain, what would you do?

Would an endless vacation for you mean Paris and Rome? Would it mean mentoring at children's clubs or serving at the local soup kitchen? Or maybe it would mean deepening your ties to those immediately around you—neighbors, friends, and family. Maybe it would mean more time to take part in the hobbies and activities you love. Have you been considering a second (or even third) act as a small-business owner, turning a hobby or passion into a revenue source?

This is your time to daydream and answer the question: If you could do anything, what would you do?

After that, it's a matter of putting a dollar amount on it. What are the costs of round-the-world travel? One couple I know said their highest priority in retirement was being able to take each of their grandchildren on a cross-country vacation every year. That's a pretty specific goal—one that is reasonably easy to nail down a budget for.

Current Budget

Compiling a current expense report is one of the trickiest pieces of retirement preparation. Many people assume the expenses of their lives in retirement will be different—lower. After all, there will be no drive to work, no need for a formal wardrobe, and, perhaps most impactful of all, no more saving for retirement!

Yet, we often underestimate our daily spending habits. That's why I typically ask my clients to bring in their bank statements for the past year—they are reflective of your *actual* spending, not just what you think you're spending.

An easy way to figure out how much you actually spend versus your monthly bills is sometimes helped if the majority of your expenses are paid from a single account. It can be a bank account or a mileage/rewards credit card. If you pay the majority of your day-to-day expenditures and bills (electric, water, cable, phone, etc.) on this one account, it's easy to show you what your current lifestyle really costs.

I'm a big fan of a rewards credit card. As long as you always pay off the card every month, you can get some valuable benefits on expenses you're going to pay anyway. It's an easy way to keep track of what you're actually spending instead of just your fixed costs.

I have been flying first class for over twenty years. It's not that I'm extravagant; I'm actually pretty frugal. It's because I have a credit card that gives me points for paying my bills through them. There is an annual fee, but the benefits outweigh the annual cost. I have flown first class for free for over twenty years just by paying expenses from a reward account instead of my bank account.

I can't count the number of times I have sat with a couple in my office, asked them about their spending, and heard them throw out a number that seemed incredibly low. When I ask them where the number came from, they usually say they estimated based on their total bills. Yet, our spending is so much more than our mortgage, utilities, cable, phone, car, grocery, or credit card bills.

"What about clothes?" I ask, "Or dining out? What about gifts and coffees and last-minute birthday cards?" That's when the lights come on.

This is why I suggest collecting a year's worth of information. There is usually no such thing as a one-time purchase. Did you buy new furniture? Even if that is a rarity, do you think that will be the last time you *ever* buy furniture?

I can't tell you how many times, people give me a figure of how much they anticipate spending in retirement, only to find out that they are currently spending two to three times that figure. They might anticipate spending less than they do currently, but my experience is that you'll spend pretty close to what you do now, if you'd like to maintain the same lifestyle. Many times, you can cut back on things like charity, the grandkids, traveling less, etc., but isn't the point of proper retirement planning to maintain your current lifestyle, not some pared down version of your lifestyle?

Another hefty expense is spending on the kids. Many of the couples I work with are quick to help their adult children, whether it's something like letting them live in the basement, paying for college, babysitting, paying an occasional bill, or contributing to a grandchild's college fund. They aren't alone—79 percent of Americans in 2018 said they had provided financial support for an adult child. And it's not unlikely for some parents to tap into their retirement funds to do so.[26]

My clients sometimes protest that what they do for their grown children can stop in retirement. They don't *need* to help. But I get it. Parents like to feel needed. And, while you never want to neglect saving for retirement in favor of taking on financial risks (like your child's student debt), the parents who help their adult children do so in part because it helps them feel fulfilled.

When it comes down to expenses, including (and especially) spending on your family, don't make your initial calculations based on what you *could* whittle your budget down to if you *had* to. Instead, start from where you are. Who wants to live off a bare-bones bank account in retirement?

Other Expenses

Once you have nailed down your current budget and your dreams or goals for retirement, there are a few other outstanding pieces to think about—some expenses many people don't take the time to consider before making and executing a plan. But I'm assuming you want to get it right, so let's take a look.

Housing

Do you know where you want to live in retirement? This makes up a substantial piece of your income puzzle—since the

---

[26] Lorie Konish. CNBC. October 2, 2018. "Parents Spend Twice as Much on Adult Children than They Save for Retirement." https://www.cnbc.com/2018/10/02/parents-spend-twice-as-much-on-adult-children-than-saving-for-retirement.html

typical American household owns a home, and it's generally their largest asset.

Some people prefer to live right where they are for as long as they can. Others have been waiting for retirement to pull the trigger on an ambitious move, like purchasing a new house, or even downsizing. Whatever your plans and whatever your reasons, there are quite a few things to consider.

Mortgage

Do you still have a mortgage? What may have been a nice tax boon in your working years could turn into a financial burden in your retirement. After all, when you are on a limited income, a mortgage is just one more bill sapping your financial strength. It is something to put some thought into, whether you plan to age in place or are considering moving to your dream home, buying a house out of state, or living in a retirement community.

Upkeep and Taxes

A house without a mortgage still requires annual taxes. While it's tempting to think of this as a once-a-year expense, when you have limited earning potential, your annual tax bill might be something into which you should put a little more forethought.

The costs of homeownership aren't just monetary. When you find yourself dealing with more house than you need, it can drain your time and energy. From keeping clutter at bay to keeping the lawn mower running, upkeep can be extensive and expensive. For some, that's a challenge they heartily accept and can comfortably take on. For others, the idea of yard work or cleaning an area larger than they need feels foolish.

For instance, Peggy discovered after her knee replacement that most of her house was inaccessible to her when she was laid up.

"It felt ridiculous to pay someone else to dust and vacuum a house I was only living in 40 percent of!"

Practicality and Adaptability

Erik and Magda are looking to retire within the next two decades. They just sold their old three-bedroom ranch-style house. Their twins are in high school, and the couple has wanted to "upgrade" for years. Now they live in a gorgeous 1940s three-story house with all the kitchen space they ever wanted, five sprawling bedrooms, and a library and media room for themselves and their children. Within months of moving in, the couple realized a house perfect for their active teens would no longer be perfect for them in five to fifteen years.

"We are paying the mortgage for this house, but we've started saving for the next one," said Magda, "because who wants to climb two flights of stairs to their bedroom when they're seventy-eight?"

Others I know have encountered a similar situation in their personal lives. After a health crisis, one couple found the luxurious tub for two they toiled to install had become a specter of a bad slip and a potential safety risk. It's important to think through what your physical reality could be. I always emphasize to my clients that they should plan for whatever their long-term future might hold, but it's amazing how many people don't give it much thought.

Contracts and Regulations

If you are looking into a cross-country move, be aware of new tax tables or local ordinances in the area where you are looking to move. After all, you don't want to experience sticker-shock when you are looking at downsizing or reducing your bills in retirement.

Along the same lines, if you are moving into a retirement community, be sure to look at the fine print. What happens if you must move into a different situation for long-term care?

Will you be penalized? Will you be responsible for replacing your slot in the community? What are all the fees, and what do they cover?

Since I've been in the business of financial and retirement planning since the 1980s, I have countless stories of people who move out of state and downsize their homes to save on property taxes only to find out they ultimately owe more in taxes as a result of a higher income tax in their new state. I also have clients who moved into a retirement community, then needed to move again a few years later because of monthly dues and shared community expenses that seem to increase every year.

One of the most common mistakes or miscalculation is the reality of "downsizing." The idea is to save money by moving to a smaller home when they retire. The kids are grown, so they don't need nearly as much space. Their thoughts are that they'll have lower utility bills and generally a lower cost of living. The issue is most people want to buy a home newer than theirs with newer appliances, fixtures, and more energy efficient features. They want to experience fewer headeaches and maintenance than an older home. A new home, even though it's smaller, is most likely more expensive than your current, larger home. You also might have had your taxes locked in when you turned sixty-five only to have them subject to new higher tax valuations at the new home.

I have clients who bought older homes, because they researched the tax history on the home and it was significantly lower than their current taxes. They later found out that the previous owners were an older couple who had their taxes frozen when they turned sixty-five over fifteen years ago. They didn't realize the taxes would reset to today's value and therefore they would have a much higher tax bill. They thought they wouldn't have the higher taxes, since they were both over age sixty-five. In some localities, property taxes can't increase when you're over sixty-five, but when a property changes hands, the value and the taxes will move up to current values.

My point with all of this is to help you understand that a lot goes into deciding where to live in retirement. There are so many issues you might not have thought existed or were that important. It's a great idea to speak to an experienced planner to ensure you have all the information for you and your family to make the best decision for your future.

Inflation

As I write this in 2021, America had experienced a long stretch of low inflation. Inflation had not exceeded 4 percent since 1991 until that 30-year run ended with readings exceeding 4 percent in April 2021.[27]

However, inflation isn't a one-time bump; it has a cumulative effect. Even with relatively low inflation over the past few decades, the $20 sneakers you bought your grade-schooler in 1991 will cost $37.90 to buy for your grandchild today.[28] What if, in retirement, we hit a stretch like the late seventies and early eighties, when annual inflation rates of 10 percent became the norm? It may be wise to consider some extra padding in your retirement income plan to account for any potential increase in inflation in the future.

Aging

Also, in the expense category, think about longevity. We all hope to age gracefully. However, it's important to face the prospect of aging with a sense of realism.

The elephant in the room for many families is long-term care: No one wants to admit they will likely need it, but estimates say as many as 70 percent of us will. [29] Aging is a

---

[27] US Inflation Calculator. January 2021. "Historical Inflation Rates." http://www.usinflationcalculator.com/inflation/historical-inflation-rates/
[28] Ibid.
[29] Moll Law Group. 2021. "The Cost of Long-Term Care." https://www.molllawgroup.com/the-cost-of-long-term-care.html

significant piece of retirement income planning because you'll want to figure out how to set aside money for your care, either at home or away from it. The more comfortable you get with discussing your wishes and plans with your loved ones, the easier planning for the financial side of it can be.

I discuss health care and potential long-term care costs in more detail elsewhere in this book, but suffice it to say nursing home care tends to be very expensive and typically isn't something you get to choose when you will need.

It isn't just the costs of long-term care that pose a concern in living longer. It's also about covering the possible costs of everything else associated with living longer. For instance, if Henry retires from his job as a biochemical engineer at age sixty-five, perhaps he planned to have a very decent income for twenty years, until age eighty-five. But what if he lives until he's ninety-five? That's a whole third—ten years—more of personal income he will need.

Putting It All Together

Whew! So, you have pulled together what you have, and you have a pretty good idea of where you want to be. Now your financial professional and you can go about the work of arranging what assets you *have* to cover what you *need*—and how you might try to cover any gaps.

Like the proverbial man in the Bible who built his house on a rock, I like to help my clients figure out how to cover their day-to-day living expenses—their needs—with insurance and other guaranteed income sources like pensions and Social Security.

We use detailed planning software combined with decades of experience to give you a comprehensive view of a potential retirement. If you can start this process within ten or fifteen years of retirement, you can easily identify problem areas and make adjustments. The earlier you plan, the less painful the adjustments. We then "stress test" the results. We want to help ensure that increasing taxes, inflation, a bear market, prolonged poor interest rates, or anything else won't derail your retirement plans. With this type of road map, you can be content your retirement has been built to help ensure you're fiscally sound no matter what life throws at you.

Again, you should keep in mind there isn't one single financial vehicle, asset, or source to fill all your needs, and that's okay. One of the challenges of planning for your income in retirement concerns figuring out what products and strategies to use. You can release some of that stress when you accept the fact you will probably need a diverse portfolio—potentially with bonds, stocks, insurance, and other income sources—not just one massive money pile.

One way to help shore up your income gaps is by working with your financial professional and a qualified tax advisor to mitigate your tax exposure. If you have a 401(k) or IRA, a tax advisor in your corner can help you figure out how and when to take distributions from your account in a way that doesn't push you into a higher tax bracket. Or you might learn how to use tax-advantaged bonds more effectively. Effective tax planning isn't necessarily about "adding" to your income. Especially regarding retirement, it's less about what you make than it is about what you keep. Paying a lower tax bill keeps more money in your pocket, which is where you want it when it comes to retirement income.

Now you can look at ways to cover your remaining retirement goals. Are there products like long-term care insurance specific to a certain kind of expense you anticipate? Is there a particular asset you want to use for your "play" money—money for trips and gifts for the grandkids? Is there any way you can portion off money for those charitable legacy plans?

Once you have analyzed your income wants, needs, and the assets to realistically cover them, you may have a gap. The masterstroke of a competent financial professional will be to help you figure out how you will cover that gap. Will you need to cut out a round of golf a week? Maybe skip the new car? Or will you need to take more substantial action?

One way to cover an income gap is to consider working longer or even part-time before retirement and even after that magical calendar date. This may not be the best "plan" for you; disabilities, work demands, and physical or emotional limitations can hinder the best-laid plans to continue working. However, if it is physically possible for you, this is one considerable way to help your assets last, for more than one reason.

In fact, there are 10.6 million Americans in the workforce over the age of sixty-five. More than 25 percent of people in the sixty-five to seventy-four age group are still working, as well as 8.9 percent of people over seventy-five.[30]

When you're retired, you no longer have an employer paying you a steady check. It is up to you to make sure you have saved and planned for the income you need.

Some clients come into my office wanting to retire and leave the stress of their job behind, but are unsure if they're in a position to do so financially. By compiling all their information and stress testing the results, we sometimes find they could comfortably retire now without many issues.

By keeping expenses low and securing a sufficient income stream to supplement Social Security, even couples who had a large number in their heads before retiring may already have more than enough to live a comfortable lifestyle.

Everyone is different. Some people want to work forever. Some people can't wait for the day they can retire. With proper planning, at least you will know exactly what you can and can't do. Then, you can decide when and where to retire on your terms.

---

[30] Julie Jason. Forbes. Nov. 14, 2021. "Still Working After Age 65 And Thinking Of Moving?"
https://www.forbes.com/sites/juliejason/2021/11/14/still-working-after-age-65-and--thinking-of-moving/?s1=1dfff8e85402

CHAPTER 5

401(k)s & IRAs

H ave you heard? Today's retirement is not your parents' retirement. You see, back in the day, it was pretty common to work for one company for the vast majority of your career and then retire with a gold watch and a pension.

The gold watch was a symbol of the quality time you had put in at that company, but the pension was more than a symbol. Instead, it was a guarantee—as solid as your employer—that they would repay your hard work with a certain amount of income in your old age. Did you see the caveat there? Your pension's guarantee was *as solid as your employer*. The problem was, what if your employer went under?

Companies that failed couldn't pay their retired employees' pensions, leading to financial challenges for many. Beginning in 1974 with Congress' passage of the Employee Retirement Income Security Act, federal legislation and regulations aimed at protecting retirees were everywhere. One piece of legislation included a relatively obscure section of the Internal Revenue Code, added in 1978. Section 401(k), to be specific.

IRC section 401, subsection k, created tax advantages for employer-sponsored financial products, even if the main contributor was the employee him or herself. Over the years, more employers took note, beginning an age of transition away from pensions and toward 401(k) plans. A 401(k) is a retirement account with certain tax benefits and restrictions on the investments or other financial products inside of it.

Essentially, 401(k)s and their individual retirement account (IRA) counterparts are "wrappers" that provide tax benefits around assets; typically, the assets that compose IRAs and 401(k)s are mutual funds, stock and bond mixes, and money market accounts. However, IRA and 401(k) contents are becoming more diverse these days, with some companies offering different kinds of annuity options within their plans.

Where pensions are defined-*benefit* plans, 401(k)s and IRAs are defined-*contribution* plans. The one-word change outlines the basic difference. Pensions spell out what you can expect to receive from the plan but not necessarily how much money it will take to fund those benefits. With 401(k)s, an employer sets a standard for how much they will contribute (if any), and you can be certain of what you are contributing. Still, there is no outline for what you can expect to receive in return for those contributions.

Modern employment looks very different. A 2018 survey by the Bureau of Labor Statistics determined U.S. workers stayed with their employers a median of about four years. Workers ages fifty-five to sixty-four had a little more staying power and were most likely to stay with their employer for about ten years.[31] Additionally, the outlook on the benefits front is different today, too. In 1979, 38 percent of workers had pensions. But 401(k)s are rising in number, with about 55 million American workers enrolled in a plan.[32]

A far cry from a pension and gold watch, wouldn't you say?

Planning for retirement with a significant pension is vastly different. Typically, a combination of a significant pension and Social Security will pay the majority of expenses for a typical retiree. A pensioner doesn't have the burden of paying

---

[31] Bureau of Labor Statistics. September 20, 2018. "Employee Tenure Summary." https://www.bls.gov/news.release/tenure.nro.htm

[32] Investment Company Institute. December 31, 2018. "Frequently Asked Questions about 401(k) Plan Research." https://www.ici.org/policy/retirement/plan/401k/faqs_401k

expenses throughout their lifetime, so the asset allocation can be much different than someone without a pension.

Planning is much more crucial for those who don't have a significant pension or need more income than Social Security and the pension will provide. Assets must be allocated in a way to help ensure your lifestyle can be maintained as long as you may live. You need your investments to produce predictable steady income. Being too aggressive or conservative at this juncture might be the recipe for retirement disaster.

If there is anything to learn from the paradigm shift away from pensions, it's that you must look out for yourself. Whether you have worked for a company for two years or twenty, you are still the one who has to look out for your own best interests. That holds doubly true when it comes to preparing for retirement. If you are one of the lucky ones who still has a pension, good for you. But for the rest of us, it is likely a 401(k)—or possibly one of its nonprofit- or government-sector counterparts, a 403(b) or 457 plan—is one of your biggest assets for retirement.

Some employers offer incentives to contribute to their company plans, like a company match. On that subject, I have one thing to say: *Do it!* Nothing in life is free, as they say, but a company match on your retirement funds is about as close to free money as it gets. If you can make the minimum to qualify for your company's match at all, go for it.

Now, it's likely, during our working years, we mostly "set and forget" our 401(k) funding. Because it is tax-advantaged, your employer is taking money from your paycheck—before taxes—and putting it into your plan for you. Maybe you got to pick a selection of investments, or maybe your company only offers one choice of investment in your 401(k). Either way, while you are gainfully employed, your most impactful decision may just be the decision to continue funding your plan in the first place. But, when you are ready to retire or move jobs, you have choices to make requiring a little more thought and care.

When you are ready to part ways with your job, you have a few options:

- Leave the money where it is
- Take the cash (and pay income taxes and perhaps a 10 percent additional federal tax if you are younger than age fifty-nine-and-one-half)
- Transfer the money to another employer plan (if the new plan allows)
- Roll the money over into a self-directed IRA

Now, these are just general options. You will have to decide, hopefully with the help of a financial professional, what's right for you. For instance, 401(k)s are typically pretty closely tied to the companies offering them, so when changing jobs, it may not always be possible to transfer a 401(k) to another 401(k). Leaving the money where it is may also be out of the question—some companies have direct cash payout or rollover policies once someone is no longer employed.

Also, remember what we said earlier about how we change jobs more often these days? That means you likely have a 401(k) with your current company, but you may also have a string of retirement accounts trailing you from other jobs.

I have many instances of clients or friends who forgot they had an old 401(k) with a previous employer. They may have only worked there a short time or they didn't remember contributing to a 401(k). Some employers, like myself, contribute money to their employees' 401(k)s whether the employee contributes or not. It's always best to do the research contacting your former employers to ensure you don't have any assets you weren't aware of.

When it comes to your retirement income, it's important to be able to pull together *all* your assets, so you can examine what you have and where, and then decide what you will do with it.

Tax-Qualified, Tax-Preferred, Tax-Deferred ... Still TAXED

Financial media often cite IRAs and 401(k)s for their tax benefits. After all, with traditional plans, you put your money in, pre-tax, and it hopefully grows for years, even decades, untaxed. That's why these accounts are called "tax-qualified" or "tax-deferred" assets. They aren't *tax-free!* Rarely does Uncle Sam allow business to continue without receiving his piece of the pie, and your retirement assets are no different. If you didn't pay taxes on the front end, you will pay taxes on the money you withdraw from these accounts in retirement. Don't get me wrong: This isn't an inherently good or bad thing; it's just the way it is. It's important to understand, though, for the sake of planning ahead.

In retirement, many people assume they will be in a lower tax bracket. Are you planning to pare down your lifestyle in retirement? Perhaps you are, and perhaps you will have substantially less income in retirement. But many of my clients tell me they want to live life more or less the same as they always have. The money they would previously have spent on business attire or gas for their commute they now want to spend on hobbies and grandchildren. That's all fine, and for many of them, it is doable, but does it put them in a lower tax bracket? Probably not.

Keep in mind, IRAs, 401(k)s, and their alternatives have a few limitations because of their special tax status. For one thing, the IRS sets limits on your contributions to these retirement accounts. If you are contributing to a 401(k) or an equivalent nonprofit or government plan, your annual contribution limit is $19,500 (as of 2021). If you are fifty or older, the IRS allows additional contributions, called "catch-up contributions," of up to $6,500 on top of the regular limit of $19,500.[33] For an IRA, the limit is $6,000, with a catch-up limit of an additional $1,000.[34]

Because their tax advantages come from their intended use as retirement income, withdrawing funds from these accounts before you turn fifty-nine-and-one-half can carry stiff penalties. In addition to fees your investment management company might charge, you will have to pay income tax *and* a 10 percent federal tax penalty, with few exceptions.

The fifty-nine-and-one-half rule for retirement accounts is incredibly important to remember, especially when you're young. Younger workers are often tempted to cash out an IRA from a previous employer and then are surprised to find their checks missing 20 percent of the account value to income taxes, penalty taxes, and account fees.

Many millennials I see in my practice say, while they may be socking money away in their workplace retirement plan, it is often the *only* place they are saving. This could be problematic later because of the fifty-nine-and-one-half rule; what if you have an emergency? It is important to fund your retirement, but you need to have some liquid assets handy as emergency funds. This can help you avoid breaking into your retirement accounts and incurring taxes and penalties because of the fifty-nine-and-one-half rule.

RMDs

Remember how we talked about the 401(k) or IRA being a "tax wrapper" for your funds? Well, eventually, Uncle Sam will want a bite of that candy bar. So, when you turn seventy-two, the government requires you withdraw a portion of your

---

[33] Jackie Stewart. Kiplinger.com. February 5, 2021. "401(k) Contribution Limits for 2021" https://www.kiplinger.com/retirement/retirement-planning/602191/401k-contribution-limits-for-2021#:~:text=The%20maximum%20amount%20workers%20can,contributions%20for%202021%20to%20%2426%2C000
[34] Fidelity.com. 2021. "IRA contribution limits" https://www.fidelity.com/retirement-ira/contribution-limits-deadlines

account, which the IRS calculates based on the size of your account and your estimated lifespan. This required minimum distribution, or RMD, is the government's insurance it will collect some taxes, at some point, from your earnings. Because you didn't pay taxes on the front end, you will now pay income taxes on whatever you withdraw, including your RMDs. Also, let me just remind you not to play chicken with the U.S. government; if you don't take your RMDs starting at seventy-two, you will have to write a check to the IRS for *50 percent* of the amount of your missed RMDs. With the change in law from the SECURE Act of 2019, even after you begin RMDs, you can still also continue contributing to your 401(k) or IRAs if you are still employed, which can affect the whole discussion on RMDs and possible tax considerations.

If you don't need income from your retirement accounts, RMDs can seem like more of a tax burden than an income boon. While some people prefer to reinvest their RMDs, this comes with the possibility of additional taxation: You'll pay income taxes on your RMDs and then capital gains taxes on the growth of your investments. If you are legacy minded, there are other ways to use RMDs, many of which have tax benefits.

Permanent Life Insurance
One way to turn those pesky RMDs into a legacy is through permanent life insurance. Assuming you need the death benefit coverage and can qualify for it medically, if properly structured, these products can pass on a sizeable death benefit to your beneficiaries, tax-free, as part of your general legacy plan.

ILIT
Another way to use RMDs toward your legacy is to work with an estate planning attorney to create an irrevocable life insurance trust (ILIT). This is basically a permanent life insurance policy placed within a trust. Because the trust is

irrevocable, you would relinquish control of it, but, unlike with just a permanent life insurance policy, your death benefit won't count toward your taxable estate.

Annuities

Because annuities can be tax-deferred, using all or a portion of your RMDs to fund an annuity contract can be one way to further delay taxation while guaranteeing your income payments (either to you or your loved ones) later. (Assuming you don't need the RMD income during your retirement.)

Qualified Charitable Distributions

If you are charity-minded, you may use your RMDs toward a charitable organization instead of using them for income. You must do this directly from your retirement account (you can't take the RMD check and *then* pay the charity) for your withdrawals to be qualified charitable distributions (QCDs), but this is one way of realizing some of the benefits of a charitable legacy during your own lifetime. You will not need to pay taxes on your QCDs, and they won't count toward your annual charitable tax deduction limit, plus you'll be able to see how the organization you are supporting uses your donations. You should consult a financial professional on how to correctly make a QCD, particularly since the SECURE Act of 2019 has implemented a few regulations on this point.[35]

I help people reallocate assets with the goal of lowering their income under certain tax brackets to ensure the smallest taxation of their RMDs. A lot of people don't realize they can take money out of IRAs for little or no taxes, if they can keep their overall income below certain thresholds. Keep in mind, I'm not an accountant and you should always consult with

---

[35] Bob Carlson. Forbes. January 28, 2020. "More Questions And Answers About The SECURE Act."
https://www.forbes.com/sites/bobcarlson/2020/01/28/more-questions-and-answers-about-the-secure-act/#113d49564869

your tax professional before implementing any type of tax reduction strategy.

Roth IRA

Since the Taxpayer Relief Act of 1997, there has been a different kind of retirement account, or "tax wrapper," available to the public: the Roth. Roth IRAs and Roth 401(k)s each differ from their traditional counterparts in one big way: You pay your taxes on the front end. This means, once your post-tax money is in the Roth account, as long as you follow the rules and limitations of that account, your distributions are truly tax-free. You won't pay income tax when you take withdrawals, so, in turn, you don't have to worry about RMDs. However, Roth accounts have the same limitations as traditional 401(k)s and IRAs when it comes to withdrawing money before age fifty-nine-and-one-half, with the added stipulation that the account must have been open for at least five years in order for the accountholder to make withdrawals.

You can convert your entire Traditional and Rollover IRA to a Roth IRA. There are also strategies to convert a portion of your IRA to a Roth IRA. This strategy consists of converting small parts of the IRA to help keep you in a lower tax bracket, ensuring you're only paying taxes in a smaller bracket, thus reallocating assets from taxable to tax free accounts without a significant tax hit. I don't often recommend converting large IRAs to Roth IRAs, because of the potentially significant tax consequences, as any amount converted is taxed in the year converted. A Roth conversion protects you from future tax increases, but the tax bite can be severe enough that it doesn't work out mathematically. There is an exception; if you're in the highest tax bracket and expect to stay in the highest bracket in retirement when the paycheck stops, then protecting yourself from potential tax increases often makes sense.

Roth IRA conversions are very popular. In my experience, people in general are concerned about tax increases, especially when they're retired, so it makes sense that we would want to protect ourselves from future tax increases. The general thinking is that tax free must be better than taxable. Right? Well, the answer is "maybe."

What you need to be concerned with is how much "after tax" you would have if you implemented a conversion. If it cost you 35 percent in taxes to convert an IRA to a Roth IRA, but your tax bracket taking out regular IRA distibutions is well under 35 percent, then a conversion probably doesn't make sense. There are other reasons for conversion, but since most of us are planning to be in a lower tax bracket during retirement, since the paycheck stopped, it doesn't make mathematical sense for a large lump sum conversions for many IRA owners. The only way to know for sure is to run the numbers.

Taking Charge

As mentioned earlier, the 401(k) and IRA have largely replaced pensions, but they aren't an equal trade.

Pensions are employer-funded; the money feeding into them is money that wouldn't ever show up on your pay stub. Because 401(k)s are self-funded, you must actively and consciously save. This distinction has made a difference when it comes to funding retirement. According to one NerdWallet article, the average 401(k) balance for a person age sixty to sixty-nine is $198,600, but the median likely tells the full story. The median 401(k) balance for a person age sixty to sixty-nine is $63,000. The article also cites the general suggestion to aim, by age thirty, to have saved up an amount equal to 50 percent to 100 percent of your annual salary.[36] For

---

[36] Arielle O'Shea. Nerd Wallet. March 17, 2021. "The Average 401(k) Balance by Age." https://www.nerdwallet.com/article/investing/the-average-401k-balance-by-age

some thirty-year-olds, saving half an annual salary by age thirty is more than some sixty-to-sixty-nine-year-olds have saved for their entire lives

There can be many reasons why people underfund their retirement plans, like being overwhelmed by the investment choices or taking withdrawals from IRAs when they leave an employer, but the reason at the top of the list is this: People simply aren't participating to begin with.

So, whether you use a 401(k) with an employer or an IRA alternative with a private company, separate from your workplace, the most important retirement savings decision you can make is to sock away your money somewhere in the first place.

CHAPTER 6

Social Security

S ocial Security is often the foundation of retirement income. Backed by the strength of the U.S. Treasury, it provides perhaps the most dependable paycheck you will have in retirement.

From the time you collect your first paycheck from the job that made you a bonafide taxpayer (for me, it was working as a busboy at the Windjammer restaurant in Garland, Texas), you are paying into the grand old Social Security system. What grew and developed out of the pressures of the Great Depression has become one of the most popular government programs in the country, and, if you pay in for the equivalent of ten years or more, you, too, can benefit from the Social Security program.

Now, before we get into the nitty-gritty of Social Security, I'd like to address a current concern: Will Social Security still be there for you when you reach retirement age?

The Future of Social Security

This question is ever-present as headlines trumpet an underfunded Social Security program, alongside the sea of baby boomers who are retiring in droves and the comparatively smaller pool of younger people who are bearing the responsibility of funding the system.

The Social Security Administration itself acknowledges this concern as each Social Security statement now bears an asterisk that continues near the end of the summary:

> *"*Your estimated benefits are based on current law. Congress has made changes to the law in the past and can do so at any time. The law governing benefit amounts may change because, by 2034, the payroll taxes collected will be enough to pay only about 79 percent of scheduled benefits."*

Just a reminder, as if you needed one, that nothing in life is guaranteed. Additionally, depending on who you're listening to, Social Security funds may run low before 2034 thanks to the financial instability and government spending that accompanied the 2020 COVID-19 pandemic.

Before you get too discouraged, though, here are a few thoughts to keep you going:

- Even if the program is only paying 79 cents on the dollar for scheduled benefits, 79 percent is notably not zero.
- The Social Security Administration has made changes in the distant and near past to protect the fund's solvency, including increasing retirement ages and striking certain filing strategies.
- There are many changes Congress could make, and lawmakers are currently discussing how to fix the system, such as further increasing full retirement age and eligibility.
- One thing no one is seriously discussing? Reneging on current obligations to retirees or the soon-to-retire.

Take heart. The real answer to the question, "Will Social Security be there for me?" is still yes.

This question is an important one to consider when you look at how much we, as a nation, rely on this program. Did you know Social Security benefits replace about 40 percent of a person's original income when they retire?[37]

If you ask me, that's a pretty significant piece of your retirement income puzzle.

Another caveat? You may not realize this, but no one can legally "advise" you about your Social Security benefits.

"But, Victor," you may be thinking, "isn't that part of what you do? And what about that nice gentleman at the Social Security Administration office I spoke with on the phone?"

Don't get me wrong. Social Security Administration employees know their stuff. They are trained to know policies and programs, and they are usually pretty quick to tell you what you can and cannot do. But the government specifically says, because Social Security is a benefit you alone have paid into and earned, your Social Security decisions, too, are yours alone.

When it comes to financial professionals, we can't push you in any directions, either, *but*—there's a big but here—working with a well-informed financial professional is still incredibly handy when it comes to your Social Security decisions. Why? Because someone who's worth his or her salt will know what withdrawal strategies might pertain to your specific situation and will ask questions that can help you determine what you are looking for when it comes to your Social Security.

For instance, some people want the highest possible monthly benefit. Others want to start their benefits early, not always because of financial need. I heard about one man who called in to start his Social Security payments the day he qualified, just because he liked to think of it as the government paying back a debt it owed him, and he enjoyed the feeling of receiving a check from Uncle Sam.

Whatever your reasons, questions, or feelings regarding Social Security, the decision is yours alone; but working with a financial professional can help you put your options in

---

[37] Social Security Administration. "Learn About Social Security Programs." https://www.ssa.gov/planners/retire/r&m6.html

perspective by showing you—both with industry knowledge and with proprietary software or planning processes—where your benefits fit into your overall strategy for retirement income.

One reason the federal government doesn't allow for "advice" related to Social Security, I suspect, is so no one can profit from giving you advice related to your Social Security benefit—or from providing any clarifications. Again, this is a sign of a good financial professional. Those who are passionate about their work will be knowledgeable about what benefit strategies might be to your advantage and will happily share those possible options with you.

Full Retirement Age

When it comes to Social Security, it seems like many people only think so far as "yes." They don't take the time to understand the various options available. Instead, because it is common knowledge you can begin your benefits at age sixty-two, that's what many of us do. While more people are opting to delay taking benefits, age sixty-two is still firmly the most popular age to start.[38]

What many people fail to understand is, by starting benefits early, they may be leaving a lot of money on the table. You see, the Social Security Administration bases your monthly benefit on two factors: your earnings history and your full retirement age (FRA).

From your earnings history, they pull the thirty-five years you made the most money and use a mathematical indexing formula to figure out a monthly average from those years. If you paid into the system for less than thirty-five years, then every year you didn't pay in will be counted as a zero.

---

[38] Chris Kissell. moneytalknews.com. January 20, 2021. "This Is When the Most People Start Taking Social Security." https://www.moneytalksnews.com/the-most-popular-age-for-claiming-social-security/

Once they have calculated what your monthly earning would be at FRA, the government then calculates what to put on your check based on how close you are to FRA. FRA was originally set at sixty-five, but, as the population aged and lifespans lengthened, the government shifted FRA later and later, based on an individual's year of birth. Check out the following chart to see when you will reach FRA.[39]

---

[39] Social Security Administration. "Full Retirement Age." https://www.ssa.gov/planners/retire/retirechart.html

Age to Receive Full Social Security Benefits*	
(Called "full retirement age" [FRA] or "normal retirement age.")	
Year of Birth*	FRA
1937 or earlier	65
1938	65 and 2 months
1939	65 and 4 months
1940	65 and 6 months
1941	65 and 8 months
1942	65 and 10 months
1943-1954	66
1955	66 and 2 months
1956	66 and 4 months
1957	66 and 6 months
1958	66 and 8 months
1959	66 and 10 months
1960 and later	67
*If you were born on Jan. 1 of any year, you should refer to the previous year. (If you were born on the 1st of the month, we figure your benefit [and your full retirement age] as if your birthday was in the previous month.)	

When you reach FRA, you are eligible to receive 100 percent of whatever the Social Security Administration says is your full monthly benefit.

Starting at age sixty-two, for every year before FRA you claim benefits, your monthly check is reduced by 5 percent or more. Conversely, for every year you delay taking benefits past FRA, your monthly benefit increases by 8 percent (until age seventy—after that, there is no monetary advantage to delaying Social Security benefits). While your circumstances and needs may vary, a lot of financial professionals still urge people to at least consider delaying until they reach age seventy.

Why Wait?[40]

Taking benefits early could affect your monthly check by _____.								
62	63	64	65	FRA 66	67	68	69	70
-25%	-20%	-13.3%	-6.7%	0	+8%	+16%	+24%	+32%

My Social Security

If you are over age thirty, you have probably received a notice from the Social Security Administration telling you to activate something called "My Social Security." This is a handy way to learn more about your particular benefit options, to keep track of what your earnings record looks like, and to calculate the benefits you have accrued over the years.

Essentially, My Social Security is an online account you can activate to see what your personal Social Security picture looks like, which you can do at www.ssa.gov/myaccount. This can be extremely helpful when it comes to planning for income in

---

[40] Social Security Administration. April 2021. "Can You Take Your Benefits Before Full Retirement Age?" https://www.ssa.gov/planners/retire/applying2.html

retirement and figuring up the difference between your anticipated income versus anticipated expenses.

My Social Security is also helpful because it's a great way to see if there is a problem. For instance, I have heard of one woman who, through diligently checking her tax records against her Social Security profile, discovered her Social Security check was shortchanging her, based on her earnings history. After taking the discrepancy to the Social Security Administration, they sent her what they owed her in makeup benefits.

COLA

Social Security is a largely guaranteed piece of the retirement puzzle: If you get a statement that says to expect $1,000 a month, you can be sure you will receive $1,000 a month. But there is one variable detail, and that is something called the cost-of-living adjustment, or COLA.

The COLA is an increase in your monthly check meant to address inflation in everyday life. After all, your expenses will likely continue to experience inflation in retirement, but you will no longer have the opportunity for raises, bonuses, or promotions you had when you were working. Instead, Social Security receives an annual cost-of-living increase tied to the Department of Labor's Consumer Price Index for Urban Wage Earners and Clerical Workers, or CPI-W. If the CPI-W measurement shows inflation rose a certain amount for regular goods and services, then Social Security recipients will see that reflected in their COLA.

The COLA averages 4 percent, but in a no- or low-inflation environment, such as in 2010, 2011, and 2016, Social Security recipients will not receive an adjustment. Some view the COLA as a perk, bump, or bonus, but, in reality, it works more like this: Your mom sends you to the store with $2.50 for a gallon of milk. Milk costs exactly $2.50. The next week, you go back with that same amount, but it is now $2.52 for a gallon, so you go back to Mom, and she gives you 2 cents. You aren't bringing home more milk—it just costs more money.

So the COLA is less about "making more money" and more about keeping seniors' purchasing power from eroding when inflation is a big factor, such as in 1975, when it was 8 percent![41] Still, don't let that detract from your enthusiasm about COLAs; after all, what if Mom's solution was: "Here's the same $2.50; try to find pennies from somewhere else to get that milk!"?

Spousal Benefits

We've talked about FRA, but another big Social Security decision involves spousal benefits.

If you or your spouse has a long stretch of zeros in your earnings history—perhaps if one of you stayed home for years, caring for children or sick relatives—you may want to consider filing for spousal benefits instead of filing on your own earnings history. A spousal benefit can be up to 50 percent of the primary wage earner's benefit at full retirement age.

To begin drawing a spousal benefit, you must be at least sixty-two years old, and the primary wage earner must have already filed for his or her benefit. While there are penalties for taking spousal benefits early (you could lose up to 67.5 percent of your check for filing at age sixty-two), you cannot earn credits for delaying past full retirement age.[42]

Like I said, the spousal benefit can be a big deal for those who don't have a very long pay history, but it's important to weigh your own earned benefits against the option of withdrawing based on a fraction of your spouse's benefits.

To look at how this could play out, let's use a hypothetical couple: Mary Jane, who is sixty, and Peter, who is sixty-two.

---

[41] Social Security Administration. "Cost-Of-Living Adjustment (COLA) Information for 2021." https://www.ssa.gov/cola/

[42] Social Security Administration. "Retirement Planner: Benefits For You As A Spouse." https://www.ssa.gov/planners/retire/applying6.html

Let's say Peter's benefit at FRA, in his case sixty-six, would be $1,600. If Peter begins his benefits right now, four years before FRA, his monthly check will be $1,200. If Mary Jane begins taking spousal benefits in two years at the earliest date possible, her monthly benefits will be reduced by 67.5 percent, to $520 per month (remember, at FRA, the most she can qualify for is half of Peter's FRA benefit).

What if Peter and Mary Jane both wait until FRA? At sixty-six, Peter begins taking his full benefit of $1,600 a month. Two years later, when she reaches age sixty-six, Mary Jane will qualify for $800 a month. By waiting until FRA, the couple's monthly benefit goes from $1,720 to $2,400.

What if Peter delays until age seventy to get his maximum possible benefit? For each year past FRA he delays, his monthly benefits increase by 8 percent. This means, at seventy, he could file for a monthly benefit of $2,112. However, delayed retirement credits do not affect spousal benefits, so as soon as Peter files at seventy, Mary Jane would also file (at age sixty-eight) for her maximum benefit of $800, so their highest possible combined monthly check is $2,912.[43]

When it comes to your Social Security benefits, you obviously will want to consider whether a monthly check based on a fraction of your spouse's earnings will be comparable to or larger than your own earnings history.

Divorced Spouses

There are a few considerations for those of us who have gone through a divorce. If you 1) were married for ten years or more *and* 2) have since been divorced for at least two years *and* 3) are unmarried *and* 4) your ex-spouse qualifies to begin Social Security, you qualify for a spousal benefit based on your ex-husband or ex-wife's earnings history at FRA. A divorced

---

[43] Office of the Chief Actuary. Social Security Administration. "Social Security Benefits: Benefits for Spouses."
https://www.ssa.gov/OACT/quickcalc/spouse.html#calculator

spousal benefit is different from the married spousal benefit in one way: You don't have to wait for your ex-spouse to file before you can file yourself.[44]

For instance, Charles and Moira were married for fifteen years before their divorce, when he was thirty-six and she was forty. Moira has been remarried for twenty years, and, although Charles briefly remarried, his second marriage ended after a few years. Charles' benefits are largely calculated based on his many years of volunteering in schools, meaning his personal monthly benefit is close to zero.

Although Moira has deferred her retirement, opting to delay benefits until she is seventy, Charles can begin taking benefits calculated from Moira's work history at FRA as early as sixty-two. However, he will also have the option of waiting until FRA to collect the maximum, or 50 percent of Moira's earned monthly benefit at her FRA.

Widowed Spouses

If your marriage ended with the death of your spouse, you might claim a benefit for your spouse's earned income as his or her widow/widower, called a survivor's benefit. Unlike a spousal benefit or divorced benefits, if your husband or wife dies, you can claim his or her full benefit. Also, unlike spousal benefits, if you need to, you can begin taking income when you turn sixty. However, as with other benefit options, your monthly check will be permanently reduced for withdrawing benefits before FRA.

If your spouse began taking benefits before he or she died, you can't delay withdrawing your survivor's benefits to get delayed credits; the Social Security Administration says you

---

44 Social Security Administration. "Retirement Planner: If You Are Divorced." https://www.ssa.gov/planners/retire/divspouse.html

can only get as much from a survivor's benefit as your deceased spouse might have gotten, had he or she lived.[45]

Taxes, Taxes, Taxes

With Social Security, as with everything, it is important to consider taxes. It may be surprising, but your Social Security benefits are not tax-free. Despite having been taxed to accrue those benefits in the first place, you may have to pay Uncle Sam income taxes on up to 85 percent of your Social Security.

The Social Security Administration figures these taxes using what they call "the provisional income formula." Your provisional income formula differs from the adjusted gross income you use for your regular income taxes. Instead, to find out how much of your Social Security benefit is taxable, the Social Security Administration calculates it this way:

Provisional Income = Adjusted Gross Income + Nontaxable Interest + ½ of Social Security

See that piece about nontaxable interest? That generally means interest from government bonds and notes. It surprises many people that, although you may not pay taxes on those assets, their income will count against you when it comes to Social Security taxation.

Once you have figured out your provisional income (also called "combined income"), you can use the following chart to figure out your Social Security taxes.[46]

---

[45] Social Security Administration. "Social Security Benefit Amounts For The Surviving Spouse By Year Of Birth." https://www.ssa.gov/planners/survivors/survivorchartred.html
[46] Social Security Administration. "Benefits Planner: Income Taxes and Your Social Security Benefits." https://www.ssa.gov/planners/taxes.html

Taxes on Social Security		
Provisional Income = Adjusted Gross Income + Nontaxable Interest − ½ of Social Security		
If you are ___ and your provisional income is___, then...		Uncle Sam will tax ___ of your Social Security
Single	Married, filing jointly	
Less than $25,000	Less than $32,000	0%
$25,000 to $34,000	$32,000 to $44,000	Up to 50%
More than $34,000	More than $44,000	Up to 85%

This is one more reason it may benefit you to work with financial and tax professionals: They can look at your entire financial picture to make your overall retirement plan as tax-efficient as possible—including your Social Security benefit.

You can reposition assets from certain income producing assets into others to help reduce or eliminate taxes on your Social Security.

Working and Social Security: The Earnings Test

If you haven't reached FRA, but you started your Social Security benefits and are still working, things get a little hairy.

Because you have started Social Security payments, the Social Security Administration will pay out your benefits (at that reduced rate, of course, because you haven't reached your FRA). Yet, because you are working, the organization must also withhold from your check to add to your benefits, which you are already collecting. See how this complicates matters?

To straighten the situation, the government has what is called the earnings test. For 2021, you can earn up to $18,960 without it affecting your Social Security check. But, for every $2 you earn past that amount, the Social Security Administration will withhold $1. The earnings test loosens in the year of your FRA; if you are reaching FRA in 2021, you can earn up to $51,540 before you run into the earnings test, and the government only withholds $1 for every $3 past that amount. The month you reach FRA, you are no longer subject to any earnings withholding. For instance, if you are still working and will turn sixty-six on December 28, 2021, you would only have to worry about the earnings test until December, and then you can ignore it entirely. Keep in mind, the money the government withholds from your Social Security benefits while you are working before FRA will be tacked back onto your benefits check after FRA.[47]

Social Security is typically an integral part of retirement planning. We use sophisticated software for every client showing various scenarios for taking benefits at different ages and in different combinations. This shows the real long-term benefits or drawbacks of taking benefits at various ages, assuming you and/or your spouse live to different ages. This allows you to make a more informed decision on your Social Security benefits.

---

[47] Social Security Administration. "Exempt Amounts Under the Earnings Test." https://www.ssa.gov/oact/cola/rtea.html

CHAPTER 7

Taxes

Where to begin with taxes? Perhaps by acknowledging we all bear responsibility for the resources we share. Roads, bridges, schools . . . It is the patriotic duty of every American to pay their fair share of taxes. Many would agree with me, though, while they don't mind paying their fair share, they're not interested in paying one cent more than that!

Now, just talking taxes probably takes your mind to April—tax season. You are probably thinking about all the forms you collect and how you file. Perhaps you are thinking about your certified public accountant or another qualified tax professional and saying to yourself, "I've already got taxes taken care of, thanks!"

However, what I see when people come into my office is that their relationship with their tax professional is purely a January through April relationship. That means they may have a tax professional, but not a tax *planner*.

What I mean is tax planning extends beyond filing taxes. In April, we are required to settle our accounts with the IRS to make sure we have paid up on our bill or to even the score if we have overpaid. But real tax planning is about making each financial move in a way that allows you to keep the most money in your pocket and out of Uncle Sam's.

Now, as a caveat, I want to emphasize I am neither a CPA nor a tax planner, but I see the way taxes affect my clients, and

I have plenty of experience helping clients implement tax-efficient strategies in their retirement plans in conjunction with their tax professionals.

It is especially important to me to help my clients develop tax-efficient strategies in their retirement plans because each dollar they can keep in their pockets is a dollar we can put to work.

In retirement, planning for taxes is just as important as planning to pay the electric bill. It's hard to survive without the lights being on, but you'll find just as much difficulty living the retirement of your dreams if you don't plan for taxes. To ensure your portfolio holds up to whatever might occur in the future, it's also a good idea to plan on taxes increasing throughout your lifetime. I believe that it's the only way you can ensure a more stress-free retirement.

The Fed

Now, in the United States, taxes can be a rather uncertain proposition. Depending on who is in the White House and which party controls Congress, we might be tempted to assume tax rates could either decline or increase in the next four to eight years accordingly. However, there is one (large!) factor we, as a nation, must confront: the national debt.

Currently, according to USDebtClock.org, we are over $26,500,000,000,000 in debt and climbing. That's $26.5 *trillion* with a "T." With just $1 trillion, you could park it in the bank at a zero percent interest rate and spend more than $54 million every day for fifty years without hitting a zero balance.

Even if Congress got a handle and stopped that debt from its daily compound, divided by each taxpayer, we each would owe about $214,000. So, will that be check or cash?

My point here isn't to give you anxiety. I'm just saying, even with the rosiest of outlooks on our personal income tax rates, none of us should count on low tax rates for the long term. Instead, you and your network of professionals (tax, legal, and financial) should constantly be looking for ways to take advantage of tax-saving opportunities as they come. After all, the best "luck" is when proper planning meets opportunity.

So, how can we get started?

Know Your Limits

One of the foundational pieces of tax planning is knowing what tax bracket you are in, based on your income after subtracting pre-tax or untaxed assets. Your income taxes are based on your taxable income.

One reason to know your taxable income and your income tax rate is so you can see how far away you are from the next lower or higher tax bracket. This is particularly important when it comes to decisions such as gifting and Roth IRA rollovers.

For instance, based on the 2021 tax table, Mallory and Ralph's taxable income is just over $330,000, putting them in the 32 percent tax bracket and about $3,400 above the upper end of the 24 percent tax bracket. They have already maxed out their retirement funds' tax-exempt contributions for the year. Their daughter, Gloria, is a sophomore in college. This couple could shave a considerable amount off their tax bill if they use the $3,400 to help Gloria out with groceries and school—something they were likely to do, anyway, but now can deliberately be put to work for them in their overall financial strategy.

Now, I use Mallory and Ralph only as an example—your circumstances are probably different—but I think this nicely illustrates the way planning ahead for taxes can save you money.

Assuming a Lower Tax Rate

Many people anticipate being in a lower tax bracket in retirement. It makes sense: You won't be contributing to retirement funds; you'll be drawing from them. And you won't have all those work expenses—work clothes, transportation, lunch meetings, etc.

Yet, do you really plan on changing your lifestyle after retirement? Do you plan to cut down on the number of times you eat out, scale back vacations, and skimp on travel?

What I see in my office is many couples spend more in the first few years, or maybe the first decade, of retirement. Sure, that may taper off later on, but usually only just in time for their budget to be hit with greater health and long-term care expenses. Do you see where this is going? Many people plan as though their taxable income will be lower in retirement and are surprised when the tax bills come in and look more or less the same as they used to. It's better to plan for the worst and hope for the best, wouldn't you agree?

401(k)/IRA

One sometimes-unexpected piece of tax planning in retirement concerns your 401(k) or IRA. Most of us have one of these accounts or an equivalent. Throughout our working lives, we pay in, dutifully socking away a portion of our earnings in these tax-deferred accounts. There's the rub: tax-deferred. Not tax-free. Very rarely is anything free of taxation when you get down to it. Using 401(k)s and IRAs in retirement is no different. The taxes the government deferred when you were in your working years are now coming due, and you will pay taxes on that income at whatever your current tax rate is.

Just to ensure Uncle Sam gets his due, the government also has a required minimum distribution, or RMD, rule. Beginning at age seventy-two, you are required to withdraw a certain minimum amount every year from your 401(k) or IRA, or else you will face a 50 percent tax penalty on any RMD monies you should have withdrawn but didn't—and that's on top of income tax.

Of course, there is also the Roth account. You can think of the difference between a Roth and a traditional retirement account as the difference between taxing the seed and taxing the harvest. Because Roths are funded with post-tax dollars, there aren't tax penalties for early withdrawals of the principal nor are there taxes on the growth after you reach age fifty-nine-and-one-half. Perhaps best of all, there are no RMDs. Of course, you must own a Roth account for a minimum of five years before you are able to take advantage of all its features.

This is one more area where it pays to be aware of your tax bracket. Some people may find it advantageous to "convert" their traditional retirement account funds to Roth account funds in a year during which they are in a lower tax bracket. Others may opt to put any excess RMDs from their traditional retirement accounts into other products, like stocks or insurance.

Does that make your head spin? Understandable. That's why it's so important to work with a financial professional and tax planner who can help you not only execute these sorts of tax-efficient strategies but also help you understand what you are doing and why.

CHAPTER 8

Estate & Legacy

I n my practice, I devote a significant portion of my time to matters of estates. That doesn't mean drawing up wills or trusts or putting together powers of attorney or anything like that. After all, I'm not an estate planning attorney. But I am a financial professional, and what part of the "estate" isn't affected by money matters?

I've included this chapter because I have seen many people do estate planning wrong. Clients, or clients' families, have come in after experiencing a death in the family and have found themselves in the middle of probate, high taxes, or a discovery of something unforeseen (often long-term care) draining the estate.

I have also seen people do estate planning right: clients or families who visit my office to talk about legacies and how to make them last and adult children who have room to grieve without an added burden of unintended costs, without stress from a family ruptured because of inadequate planning.

I'll share some of these stories here. However, I'm not going to give you specific advice, since everyone's situation is unique. I only want to give you some things to think about and to underscore the importance of planning ahead.

You Can't Take It With You

When it comes to legacy and estate planning, the most important thing is to *do it*. I have heard people from clients to celebrities (rap artist Snoop Dogg comes to mind) say they aren't interested in what happens to their assets when they die because they'll be dead. That's certainly one way to look at it. But I think that's a very selfish way to go about things—we all have people and causes we care about, and those who care about us. Even if the people we love don't *need* what we leave behind, they can still be fined or legally tied up in the probate process or burial costs if we don't plan for those. And that's not even considering what happens if you become incapacitated at some point while you are still alive. Having a plan in place can greatly reduce the stress of those responsibilities on your loved ones; it's just a loving thing to do.

Documents

There are a few documents that lay the groundwork of legacy planning. You've probably heard of all or most of them, but I'd like to review what they are and how people commonly use them. These are all things you should talk about with an estate planning attorney to establish your legacy.

Powers of Attorney

A power of attorney, or POA, is a document giving someone the authority to act on your behalf and in your best interests. These come in handy in situations where you cannot be present (think a vacation where you get stuck in Canada) or, for durable powers of attorney, even when you are incapacitated (think in a coma or coping with dementia).

It is important to have powers of attorney in place and to appoint someone you trust to act on your behalf in these matters. Have you ever heard of someone who was incapacitated after a car accident, whether from head trauma or being in a coma for weeks—sometimes months? Do you think their bills stopped coming due during that time? I like my phone company and my bank, but neither one is about to put a moratorium on sending me bills, particularly not for an extended or interminable period. A power of attorney would have the authority to pay your mortgage or cancel your cable while you are unable.

You can have multiple POAs and require them to act jointly.

What this looks like: Do you think two heads are better than one? One man, Chris, significantly relied on his two sons' opinions for both his business and personal matters. He appointed both sons as joint POA, requiring both their signoffs for his medical and financial matters.

You can have multiple POAs who can act independently.

What this looks like: Irene had three children with whom she routinely stayed. They lived in different areas of the country, which she thought was an advantage; one month she might be hiking out West, the next she could enjoy the newest off-Broadway production, and the next she could soak up some Southern sun. She named her three children as independently authorized POAs, so, if something happened, no matter where she was, the child closest could step in to act on her behalf.

You can have POAs who have different responsibilities.

What this looks like: Although Luke's friend Claire, a nurse, was his go-to and POA for health-related issues, financial matters usually made her nervous, so he appointed his good neighbor, Matt, as his POA in all of his financial and legal matters.

In addition to POAs, it may be helpful to have an advanced medical directive. This is a document where you have pre-decided what choices you would make about different health scenarios. An advanced medical directive can help ease the burden for your medical POA and loved ones, particularly when it comes to end-of-life care.

A medical directive is a very personal issue. I can't imagine not being able to live without the assistance of a machine. I wouldn't want my loved ones to have to make those kinds of decisions, so it might make sense in my case to have some kind of directive if that were to ever occur. Others might believe the opposite, which is completely understandable.

Wills

Perhaps the most basic document of legacy planning, a will is a legal document wherein you outline your wishes for your estate. When it comes to your estate after your death, having a will is the foundation of your legacy. Without one, your loved ones are left behind, guessing what you would have wanted, and the court will likely split your assets according to the state's defaults. Maybe that's exactly what you wanted, as far as anyone knows, right? Because even if you told your nephew he could have your car he's been driving, if it's not in writing, it still might go to the brother, sister, son, or daughter to whom you aren't speaking.

However, it may not be enough just to have a will. Even with a will, your assets will be subject to probate. Probate is what we call the state's process for determining a will's validity. A judge will go through your will to question if it conflicts with state law, if it is the most up-to-date document, if you were mentally competent at the time it was in order, etc. For some, this is a quick, easily-resolved process. For others, particularly if someone steps forward to contest the will, it may take years to settle, all the while subjecting the assets to court costs and attorney's fees.

One other undesirable piece of the probate process is that it is a public process. That means anyone can go to the courthouse, ask for copies of the case, and discover your assets. They can also see who is slated to receive what and who is disputing.

Going through probate with a will can be a long, painful process. Going through probate without a will can be much worse. The state will decide where your assets go. That's why having as much of your assets as possible in investments or types of accounts that avoid probate is crucial.

I have a client whose husband passed away unexpectedly at a fairly young age in his early fifties. Every asset from accounts that avoid probate like retirement accounts, payable on death (POD) accounts, annuities, and life insurance passed to her pretty quickly and painlessly. Other assets like real estate and other real assets did not. His parents didn't care for his wife, so they sued the estate, so she would not get the remaining assets. She is stuck paying taxes and upkeep on these assets until it's settled. She has mounting attorney fees.

At the writing of this book, the process continues many years later. A proper will or trust could have alleviated this burden for this widow. I'm confident the deceased husband had no idea he would pass so suddenly and I'm sure he didn't want his wife to have to endure years of pain and suffering.

It reinforces my belief that having your financial house in order should go beyond the grave. You never know when tragedy could strike. Your spouse and your family will go through enough if you pass. They're already going to experience unthinkable pain and anguish if you pass. Don't let them have to go through financial difficulties as well, because you failed to plan properly.

It's also important to remember beneficiary lines trump wills. So, that large life insurance policy? What if, when you bought it fifteen years ago, you wrote your ex-husband's name on the beneficiary line? Even if you stipulate otherwise in your will, the company that holds your policy will pay out to your ex-spouse. Or, how about the thousands of dollars in your IRA you dedicated to the children thirty years ago, but one of your children was killed in a car accident, leaving his wife and two toddlers behind? That IRA is going to transfer to your remaining children, with nothing for your daughter-in-law and grandchildren.

That may paint a grim portrait, but I can't underscore enough the importance of working with a skilled estate planning attorney to keep your will and beneficiary lines up to date as your life changes, for the sake of your loved ones.

Celebrities may seem larger than life, but they're not above making mistakes that impact their loved ones after they pass away. There have been dozens of celebrities, from singers like Sonny Bono and Prince, to actors, like Paul Walker and Philip Seymour Hoffman, who have passed without good estate plans in place, and the issues that arose as a result flooded the media.

Simple estate planning techniques can make all the difference in helping your family resolve your estate easily following your passing.

Trusts

Another piece of legacy planning to consider is the trust.

A trust is set up through an attorney and allows a third party, or trustee, to hold your assets and determine how they will pass to your beneficiaries. Many people are skeptical of trusts because they assume trusts are only appropriate for the fabulously wealthy.

However, a simple trust may only cost $1,000 to $2,500 in attorney's fees and can avoid both the expense and publicity of probate, provide a more immediate transfer of wealth, avoid some taxes, and provide you greater control over your legacy.[48]

---

[48] Regan Rondinelli-Haberek. LegalZoom. "What is the Average Cost to Prepare a Living Trust?" https://info.legalzoom.com/average-cost-prepare-living-trust-26932.html

For instance, if you want to set aside some funds for a grandchild's college education, you can make it a requirement he or she enrolls in classes before your trust will dispense any funds. Like a will, beneficiary lines will override your trust conditions, so you must still keep insurance policies and other assets up to date.

Like any financial or legal consideration, there are many options these days beyond the simple "yes or no" question of whether to have a trust. For one thing, you will need to consider if you want your trust to be revocable (you can change the terms while you are alive) or irrevocable (can't be changed; you are no longer the "owner" of the contents). A brief note here about irrevocable trusts: Although they have significant and greater tax benefits, they are still subject to a Medicaid look-back period. This means, if you transfer your assets into an irrevocable trust in an attempt to shelter them from a Medicaid spend-down, you will be ineligible for Medicaid coverage of long-term care for five years. Yet, an irrevocable trust can avoid both probate and estate taxes, and it can even protect assets from legal judgments against you.

Another thing to remember when it comes to trusts, in general, is, even if you have set up a trust, you must remember to fund it. In my thirty-four years' work, I've had numerous clients come to me, assuming they have protected their assets with a trust. When we talk about taxes and other pieces of their legacy, it turns out they never retitled any assets or changed any paperwork on the assets they wanted in the trust. So, please remember, a trust is just a bunch of fancy legal papers if you haven't followed through on retitling your assets.

Taxes

Although charitable contributions, trusts, and other tax-efficient strategies can reduce your tax bill, it's unlikely your estate will be passed on entirely tax-free. Yet, when it comes to building a legacy that can last for generations, taxes can be one of the heaviest drains on the impact of your hard work.

For 2017, the federal estate exemption was $5.49 million per individual and $10.98 million for a married couple, with estates facing up to a 40 percent tax rate after that. In 2021, those limits increased to $11.7 million for individuals and $23.4 million for married couples, with the 40 percent top level gift and estate tax remaining the same. Currently, the new estate limits are set to increase with inflation until January 1, 2026, when they will "sunset" back to the inflation-adjusted 2017 limits.[49] And that's not taking into account the various state regulations and taxes regarding estate and inheritance transfers.

Another tax concern "frequent flyer": retirement accounts.

Your IRA or 401(k) can be a source of tax issues when you pass away. For one thing, taking funds from a sizeable account can trigger a large tax bill. However, if you leave the assets in the account, there are still required minimum distributions (RMDs), which will take effect even after you die. If you pass the account to your spouse, he or she can keep taking your RMDs as is, or your spouse can retitle the account in his or her name and receive RMDs based on his or her life expectancy. Remember, if you don't take your RMDs, the IRS will take up to 50 percent of whatever your required distribution was, plus you will still have to pay income taxes whenever you withdraw that money. Thanks to rules enacted in 2020, anyone who inherits your IRA, with few exceptions (your spouse, a beneficiary less than ten years younger, or a disabled adult child, to name a few), will need to empty the account within ten years of your death.

Also—and this is a pretty big also—check with an attorney if you are considering putting your IRA or 401(k) in a trust. An improperly titled beneficiary form for the IRA could mean the

---

[49] Laura Sanders, Richard Rubin. The Wall Street Journal. April 8, 2021. "Estate and Gift Taxes 2020-2021: Here's What You Need to Know" https://www.wsj.com/articles/estate-and-gift-taxes-2020-2021-heres-what-you-need-to-know-11617908256

difference of thousands of dollars in taxes. This is just one more reason to work with a financial professional, one who can strategically partner with an estate planning attorney to diligently check your decisions.

Since I've been in this business since 1988, I've seen many estates pass relatively smoothly. I've seen others with issues lasting years. If your estate is in order with proper legacy planning, it will mean the world to the loved ones you leave behind.

CHAPTER 9

Finding a Financial Professional

The story I told in the first chapter about my father is one of the biggest reasons I'm so passionate about financial and retirement planning. My lifelong mission is to help people navigate through all the landmines of getting to and staying retired. Nothing saddens me more than hearing a story of a senior getting taken advantage of from some "get rich" or "too good to be true" investment scheme. My goal is to do anything I can to prevent that kind of thing from happening.

Like my father, my path to the financial services industry was anything but direct. I eventually returned to my home state of Texas and joined his practice as a commodities broker, but first, my journeys took me to distant places and professions.

Engineering a Dream

I spent six years in the military onboard the U.S.S. Enterprise out of Alameda, California, in the nuclear chemistry field. Being very proficient at math and science made it a natural choice. I was very good at my job, pretty quickly becoming a supervisor in the Chemistry and Radiological Controls Division. I considered staying in the field when I left the military in 1988, but I really wanted something different.

I couldn't imagine spending twelve hours a day in a small laboratory testing samples and adding chemicals to the power plant for the rest of my life. The only time I interacted with people, for the most part, was when I was handing the reigns over to the next shift. I've always been a "people" person, so I really wanted to give something else a shot.

There was a job opening at the Glen Rose nuclear power plant just southwest of Dallas, where I'm from, and the pay was decent, especially for the 1980s. But before looking for another job at a power plant, I thought I'd try my hand at my father's commodity brokerage firm in Dallas. Being the workaholic that I am, I left the Navy in California on a Friday and started at my dad's firm in Texas on Monday. When I started work, I had one of those "rude awakenings."

I went from a solitary existence in a laboratory to "cold calling" 100 to 200 people per day. A typical day had forty or fifty people a day telling me off, typically in a profanity-laden tirade. I remember making $100 my first month and I was starting to rethink changing careers. I overheard my father speaking to my grandmother, who was my favorite person in the world. He told her "This boy can't give away bread in a famine. I think the Navy ruined him." I buckled down and became the No. 1 broker at his office of approximately twenty-five brokers.

It only took a couple of years to realize commodities weren't for me. Imagine having someone send you $200,000 and then calling them a month later to tell them that they owed another $100,000 just to maintain the positions. My dad had that speculative gambling type of personality. I did not. I was much more conservative by nature.

That's when I started with stocks and bonds and the proper use of allocation between protection and risk. I started getting every license and credential I could. I already had the Series 3 (Futures Representative). I then passed the test for my Series 7 (General Securities Representative) and 63 (State Securities). Then came the Series 24 (General Securities Principal or Supervisor). I also got the Series 65 (Registered Investmet Advisor Representative) license and qualified for the Series 53 (Municipal Securities Principal or Supervisor). A bit later, I passed the test for the Group I (life and health) license.

Even though I didn't work for my father any longer, he told me I was wasting my time getting all of these licenses and credentials. At the time, I mainly sold stocks. In those days, there were very few financial planners. You were either a stock broker or a commodity broker. I told my father I believed we were entering the information age. My thoughts were that the general public would have more access to information in the future and generally be more educated in finance. I knew I would need more and more knowledge to stay ahead and I wanted more than just picking stocks.

Instead, I wanted to help people with *all* of their finances so they could thoroughly plan for their future, and since starting McClure Capital, that's exactly what I've done.

Adding It All Up

My professional career may have begun in a much different environment, but I believe my engineering background has really helped in my work as a financial professional. One universal lesson that applies here: Math never lies!

One of the biggest hurdles to overcome for anyone managing money is emotion. Advisors can mislead or highlight the good without emphasizing the negatives. Your emotions can keep you in a position longer than you should or leave you overexposed in one asset class, because you're more comfortable or bullish on one area or the other. I think one of the main reasons for my success all these decades is I use mathematics and probability as a guide.

There is nothing wrong with the "do it yourself" approach to financial planning. However, it's virtually impossible to separate yourself emotionally from your money. That will often lead to greed, luck, impulse buying, staying longer or shorter than is optimal for a given position, or giving into personal bias or the bias of others. Also, no matter how successful you might have been in amassing your assets, you only have experience with one person's finances—your own. An experienced financial professional has seen hundreds, if not thousands, of financial situations and knows how to plan and react in bull markets, bear markets, high interest rates, low interest rates, good and bad economies, and everything in between. That kind of insight can sometimes be crucial for long-term success.

Another consideration before tackling your finances alone: Retirement planning today is much different than in the past. For starters, pensions have all but gone away, while inflation and the use of 401(k)s continue to rise. Before the past ten or fifteen years, we had never seen interest rates as low as they are now. With government debt skyrocketing and extensive use of monetary policy, it doesn't look like rates are going to change much in the future.

In the old days, it came down to saving as much as you could, then putting the majority of the funds into a CD paying 6 to 10 percent (much higher in the late 1970s and early 1980s). Tax laws were much simpler. Longevity and healthcare costs weren't nearly as much of a concern as they are today. With so many things that need to be accounted for and so many things that can go wrong, it makes it imperative to find a competent and experience financial advisor to help you along the way.

Hopefully, by reading this book, you've come to the realization that a professional financial advisor makes sense. Now, it's imperative to find the right kind of advisor.

Pick Your Person

Everyone and their brother calls themselves financial planners or advisors. Some are legal fiduciaries and some are not. A fiduciary is someone who legally has to put your interest as a consumer ahead of their own. Although many types of financial transactions do not legally have to adhere to a fiduciary standard, I think it's a good idea to only seek advisors who have this standard when dealing with securities (stocks, bonds, etc.). In my opinion, that is typically the first place you should start.

Some financial professionals are specialized, only offering stocks, funds, bonds, or managed accounts. Some of them only offer insurance products like annuities and life insurance. If you work with someone who only offers some of the investment spectrum instead of most of the mainstream investments, they might steer you clear of any financial product they don't offer. Investments are just tools. Depending on the person, one type of investing might be a great choice, while another might be a terrible idea.

No matter what task you're working on, you need to utilize all the tools in your toolbox, and the same holds true for financial planning. An individual's risk tolerance, time horizon, and objectives will dictate what might be best for each individual client. That is why it's imperative to consider an advisor who offers and is compensated in all areas of financial planning.

The typical red flags to look out for when choosing a financial professional are lack of experience, limited product offerings, limited licensing, complaints, or blatant biases. They need experience with personal financial or retirement planning. There's a difference between the retail side and institutional side of the businesss. They both have similar licensing and education requirements, but vastly different jobs.

Think about it like this: When I was notified in 2008 that I had Renal Cell Carcinoma (kidney cancer), my general practioner offered to remove the kidney. He had the same license and was trained to be able to do this kind of thing. Instead, I went to a urologist, who was the head of oncology at one of the biggest hospitals in the area. The reason it made sense was that if I'm going under the knife, I want the most experienced person I could find who has done this procedure dozens, or possibly hundreds, of times. It didn't cost me any more to have the best instead of someone who had great intensions but only did it every once in a while.

I'm not suggesting surgery and financial planning are the same, but it is important to make sound decisions when it comes to your financial health. So wouldn't you want a competent and experienced professional operating on your portfolio?

With that in mind, pure fee-based advisors from a Registered Investment Advisor are the way to go, in my opinion. They don't get compensated for recommending a stock, exchange-traded fund, private investment, or a fund. Regardless of how you're allocated or how many trades are made in a given period, they are compensated only on the assets undermanagement based on a fee, which is usually around 1 percent per year. You can find more or less expensive. Some fee-based advisors still also earn commission based on non-securities products like life insurance or annuities.

My firm offers and is compensated on all types of traditional investing. We use a comprehensive retirement planning software and Social Security planning software to help ensure you're getting the most out of your benefit. We don't just sell products or strategies. We do a detailed analysis for every client, inputting different types of investments to show the potential real world long-term results of any recommendation. That way you know whether a stock or managed account might work well in your situation. You'll know whether adding an annuity, life insurance, or long-term care to the mix might help your overall finances.

One of my biggest pet peeves is a so-called advisor telling a client they need to be in a managed account or an annuity without knowing much of anything about their situation. A managed account or an annuity isn't right for everyone. There is so much else out there, and it must be carefully analyzed whether adding such a tool will potentially help or hurt the client in the long run.

A well-thought-out process is crucial to the long-term success of a client. Coupled with decades of experience, I believe this makes us a really good option to consider when choosing an advisor.

I hope this book served as a general introduction into my thoughts and beliefs when it comes to finances. However, there is only so much you can convey through the written word. As I mentioned above, I enjoy nothing more than getting to know my clients on a personal level and providing strategies that meet their specific needs. I welcome the opportunity to meet with anyone who has read this book to hear your thoughts and offer a second opinion on your road to retirement.

Acknowledgments

I would like to thank my father, who inspired me to write this book. I'd like to thank my family and staff for putting up with me during the process. Most of all, I'd like to thank all my clients for their continued support and friendship.

About the Author

As the President and CEO of the McClure Capital companies, Victor is focused on helping clients work toward their retirement dreams through a well-thought-out strategy for retirement income.

Victor got his start in the industry in 1988, as a commodity broker, quickly making the change to stocks/bonds and financial/retirement planning. He truly enjoys helping individuals reach their retirement dreams. Victor is a person who loves helping people and never plans on retiring. He subscribes to the philosophy, "If you love what you do, you'll never work a day in your life."

Victor owns a Registered Investment Advisor firm (McClure Capital Advisors, Inc.) and an insurance agency (McClure Capital, Inc.). He holds a Series 65 (Registered Investment Advisor Representative) license as well has life/health license (Texas License #939315). He has previously held the following licenses or credentials: Series 7, Series 24, Series 53, and Series 3.

Victor is married to his wife, Diana, and their blended family includes seven children. In his free time, he enjoys traveling, outdoor activities, and constant study. He believes you should learn something new every single day, so you'll always the best version of yourself.